DOES GOD

HEAL TODAY?

"BELOVED, I PRAY THAT YOU MAY PROSPER IN ALL
THINGS AND BE IN HEALTH, JUST AS YOUR SOUL
PROSPERS."

3 John 1:2 NKJV

Ryan Edberg

Copyright 2023 Ryan Edberg

ISBN: 9798389332539.

CONTENTS

ABOUT THE AUTHOR

Ryan Edberg is the founder of the Kingdom Movement, a parent organization to multiple platforms such as the Voice of God Conferences, the Kingdom Youth Conferences, True Beauty Women's Conferences, and Kingdom Worship Tours.

He functions as an owner/operator for many of the individual platforms inside Kingdom Movement, such as Kingdom Youth Conference, Kingdom Worship Tours and True Beauty Women's Conference.

After nearly two decades of touring with some of the most prominent Christian bands and artists in the world, Ryan achieved five No.1 singles including a worship EP as the lead singer of his rock band Silverline.

In recent years, he has formed a number of successful management-based organizations that specialize in multi-city events and tours as well as artist management. Today, Ryan is a respected leader and consultant in the world of event-based entertainment and Christian music.

Ryan has been featured on the Christian Broadcast Network, Moody Radio, American Family Radio, Point of View and in the Christian Post.

When he's not traveling and speaking, Ryan and his wife Jenny can be found in the suburbs of Nashville, Tennessee with their four children.

FORWARD

Ryan Edberg is as legitimate as anyone I've ever known. His journey is marked by tested truth, miracles, salvations, discipleship, and a love for the Word of God. Ryan has always challenged the norms and tested popular thought with biblical truth; both in practice and in preaching. What he has written here is not theory—It is Ryan's lifestyle! He lives out what he teaches in the pages of his new book *Does God Still Heal Today*. He lives healing, practices healing, teaches healing, and has seen the fruit of it in countless people.

At the time this book is being released, I have known Ryan well over two decades. We have ministered together at conferences, in jungles, nations, and churches, as well as to rockstars, celebrities, young and old, politicians, and everything in between. One thing I can say with great confidence is that Ryan believes everything he has written. Upon receiving the manuscript of this book, I read it from cover to cover and must honestly say, you are about to find great value in what you're going to read. I say this because it's worked in Ryan's and his wife Jenny's lives. What he covers in the pages ahead is an excellent material for both new believers and those tenured in a spirit-filled life. His presentation on the subject matter of healing is not only brilliant but presented in an applicable manner.

Ryan unashamedly confronts questions many believers are afraid to ask, yet they greatly desire the answers to. He, in his commonsense, yet no-nonsense style of questioning, makes the reader consider and then offers the solution. That's what I found myself doing. Considering, musing, and being edified by the solutions Ryan presents. He not only provides great questions but also great answers from the Word of God and his testimonies.

By nature, Ryan is an apologist, he is an intellectual whose style is disarming, yet crystal clear. He desires that you, the reader, simply look at hard questions and embrace the tools from the Word of God (along with the gripping testimonies he provides) to answer many questions in the area of divine healing.

The way Ryan powerfully uses his journey as a template is very potent. I say this because I can personally attest to the things he says and the stories he tells—as I was present for some of them. I've seen Ryan pray for countless numbers of people over the years, and nearly every time we talk, he has a new faith-filled story about a person who was tremendously healed or impacted by the power of God in one of his events or meetings.

You are also about to get a look at God's plan for man, and the benefits of what Jesus did from the right side of the cross. Jesus has paid for your sins and healing with His blood, and He wants what He paid for! Another way of saying this is that Jesus wants you healed more than you do. I benefited from the section where Ryan shares his revelation and insights on the Hebrew word shalom.

Ryan is a product of the gospel. He believes it works completely today the same way it did two thousand years ago. He lives, practices, and continues to grow in what he teaches you here. What this book will do for you, dear reader, is cause you to grow in faith, rise to your supernatural occasion, and have boldness for healing. You will have a fresh take on how much God wants you healed, how much you have a right to it, and the great confidence required to see it manifest in your life. Ryan believes what the Bible says about healing and by the time you're done reading this —you will likely agree with him!

I recommend this book to every believer and encourage you to take in each Scripture reference and testimony as fuel for your faith. I dare you to read this book, do what it says, meditate on the scriptural blueprint provided, and attempt to stay the same — you simply will not! Get ready to give your faith a powerful boost and become equipped, and healing will begin to manifest in your sphere of influence. Well done, Ryan! Thank you, my friend, for writing this powerful and much-needed book!

–Joseph Z
Author, Broadcaster, Prophetic Voice
JosephZ.com

ENDORSMENTS

What Passion! In his book, "Does God Still Heal," Ryan lays out a convincing exposé to convince even the unbelieving of God's ability and desire to heal in our 21st Century society. I recommend everyone purchase, read, study, and re-read this discourse to build your faith and experience God's supernatural healing power. — Dr. H. Michael Chitwood

Ryan Edberg has articulated a clear, concise, and precise path for everyday believers to see the supernatural working in their everyday lives.
—- Jason Anderson Living Word Mesa AZ

I've had the honor and privilege of traveling all over the country with Ryan Edberg as a speaker at the Kingdom Youth Conferences. I have watched Ryan live out this book in real time. Does God still heal today? Absolutely he does. And I've seen it. Standing next to Ryan we have prayed for people and seen God open deaf ears, remove cancer, mend broken bones, and restore marriages. And that was just at one conference! This book will change your life if you allow God to speak to you through it. God DOES heal today! And he wants to use YOU!
-Kelly K

REVIEW OF "DOES GOD STILL HEAL TODAY?"

In "Does God Still Heal Today?" author Ryan Edberg invites readers to embark on a spiritual journey that explores the enduring relevance of divine healing in this post-modern age. Delving into the depths of the Old and New Covenants, Edberg presents a compelling case for the continuing presence and power of healing through Jesus Christ.

The book is divided into three subdivisions of thought. In the first section, Edberg examines the roots of divine healing in the Old Testament, providing a solid foundation for understanding the concept in its historical context. By highlighting key biblical figures and their experiences with healing, the author effectively illustrates the importance of faith and obedience in accessing God's healing power.

As the narrative transitions to the New Testament in the second section, Edberg focuses on Jesus Christ's role as our Healer. Through a careful analysis of Jesus' teachings and miracles, the author demonstrates the transformative nature of divine healing in the lives of believers. This section also delves into the Covenantal promise of healing, emphasizing its enduring significance for believers today.

The third subdivision of thought in this book addresses contemporary questions and concerns surrounding divine healing. Edberg tackles common misconceptions and provides practical guidance for those seeking healing in their own lives. By drawing on modern-day testimonies, the author effectively connects the ancient doctrines of Divine healing to the realities of the 21st century.

Edberg's writing style is engaging and accessible, making complex theological concepts easy to grasp for readers of all backgrounds. His extensive knowledge of Scripture shines through in his detailed explanations, and his passion for the subject matter is evident on every page. This book will undoubtedly inspire his readers to reevaluate their understanding of divine healing and encourage them to seek a deeper relationship with God.

"Does God Still Heal Today?" is a thought-provoking and timely exploration of the enduring power and relevance of divine healing in the lives of believers. By tracing the concept from its biblical origins to its modern-day implications, Ryan Edberg offers a comprehensive and compelling argument for the continuing presence of healing through Jesus Christ. This book is a must-read for anyone interested in exploring the depths of their faith and unlocking the transformative potential of divine healing.

Rev. Dr. Wendell E. Hutchins II
Founder & Sr. Pastor, Church of Champions
Assistant General Overseer, City Harvest Network

THANKS

There are so many people in my life I want to thank for the support of the ministry God has called me into.

I want to thank my wife, Jenny, for always being there through the good and the bad, for being selfless and a hard worker.

I want to thank my 4 kids Taylor, Isaiah, Aubrey and Kylie for being great kids and understanding ministry; for allowing long weekends with dad traveling.

I want to thank my parents, Bruce and Christine Edberg, for always supporting me and without them Kingdom Youth, or anything I've done, wouldn't be possible.

I'm thankful for a great board and friends with wisdom; among whom are Joseph and Heather Zupetz, Jason and Kelly Anderson, Kemtal and Marla Glasgow, Lonnie and Sandy DuFrene.

I'm thankful for all the people and friends that have helped with Kingdom Youth including Markshimire and Chantsee Jones, Kelly K, Luke Widseth, Chris Crenshaw, Michael Chitwood, all the interns over the years, all the hundreds of pastors and churches that let me preach and support the ministry, Wendell Hutchins for opening doors and letting me connect with men of God like David Amos, Rod Parsley and the City Harvest Network.

Big thanks to Hailey Nichols for helping with the artwork! I also want to thank Andrew Wommack and his ministry that has had a powerful impact in my life.

A great big thank you to Kyra Thompson and all her hard work on this book as well. Great job editing and I recommend her to everyone needing a book edited. 540-273-2911 kyrat@live.com

INTRODUCTION

This book has been on my heart for a while and has been years in the making. This book is meant to answer questions like:

-Does God still heal today?

-Is it God's will for all to be healed?

-I believe in healing but why did I pray and nothing happened?

I will also address many more questions that I know a large part of the body of Christ is asking. I have also had all those questions before and have only found the answers when I looked to the Bible. We don't need another man's opinion on healing! We need to read and believe the Word of God. That is why this book will have lots of scripture in it and I want to walk through that scripture with you and see if we can answer some of the questions so you can start to see healing in your life and the lives of those around you. I was very frustrated as a Christian when I would read in the Word about healing but I never saw it in my life the way it was in scripture. It wasn't until I learned the things I am going to unpack in this book that I went from not seeing anything to seeing miracles almost every week. Regardless of whether I was seeing miracles or not, I was getting the results the Bible said I would. Sounds confusing; but after this book you will see what I mean. If you want to see stories in your life just like those in the Word then keep reading. I trust this book will encourage you and light a fire! Let's put all preconceived ideas away and look into God's Word!

CHAPTER 1

Any book on healing, miracles, or anything of the supernatural, needs to be grounded in scripture. Many Christians out there teach based on their opinion which they base on experiences instead of scripture. So often, as Christians, we base our view of God and scripture on our past experience instead of the Word. We shouldn't be trying to interpret scripture based on experiences but we should let scripture mold our experiences. So many Christians look for miracles, signs, and wonders, when we should be seeking God. When we seek God first, we start to see miracles, signs, and wonders.

But seek first the kingdom of God and His righteousness, and all these things shall be added to you. Therefore do not worry about tomorrow, for tomorrow will worry about its own things. Sufficient for the day is its own trouble. (Matthew 6:33, 34 NKJV)

If we keep our eyes on what really matters, breakthrough happens! The Word is what changes us and brings us healing, victory, or anything else we need. Sometimes we think the solution for our breakthrough can be found through a mathematical equation. That is not how it works. We cannot put God in a box and assume that 2+2=4 with God. He is outside of our understanding. We can, however, read His Word, let faith arise, and believe in what He says. We think if we pray the right way, we can get healed or if we are good enough, maybe God will heal us.

Everything in the Kingdom operates by faith but too often we don't know what that means or how to get it.

So then faith comes by hearing, and hearing by the word of God. (Romans 10:17 NKJV).

We are to be people that live by faith and we see in Romans that faith comes by hearing, and hearing by the word of God. It's important, if you want faith that can move mountains, to hear and believe the Word of God because it's His power that does the work. This is not about you trying to figure out what Ryan knows, but maybe I can show you what I've learned from scripture and what I've seen work in my life. Shema in Hebrew means to both hear and obey. We don't want to be just hearers of the Word but doers also!

The Beginning of Wisdom

My wife and I were in a spot years ago, wondering why the church today didn't look like the church in the Bible. Why were we praying but not seeing the same things the disciples saw? Why were we believing for a breakthrough but it never seemed to happen? Why were we praying for healing yet not even seeing a headache get better? This bothered me because I loved God and believed in His Word. If your prayer life is getting the same results as your neighbor that doesn't even believe in God, there is something wrong! We were not going to put up with that anymore! I wanted my life to look like the people of God in the Bible that walked on water, crossed the sea on dry ground, defeated armies with just a few men, outran chariots, survived lions' dens, got thrown into fiery furnaces and walked out fine, and so much more. I began to study scripture to look for patterns, listen to faith preachers, and spend time in prayer.

My people are destroyed for lack of knowledge. Because you have rejected knowledge, I also will reject you from being priest for Me; Because you have forgotten the law of your God, I also will forget your children. (Hosea 4:6 NKJV).

You see here in Hosea that people are destroyed for a lack of knowledge, or in other words, what you don't know *can* kill you. I am sure you've heard it the other way around; that what you don't know won't hurt you, but we can see from this passage that this is not how God's system works. Scripture puts the responsibility on us as Christians to get understanding. I didn't want to be someone living a normal life or even someone that wasn't seeing victory just because I didn't understand something.

My wife and I began to study and read the Word with not just our head but our heart. After a bit of good teaching, the Word began to open up to us. We started to see breakthroughs in our family and started to see healings happen all over. Before, we couldn't even get a headache to leave no matter how long we asked God to take it away, but now we would pray with people and see amazing miracles. It was all because we changed our thinking and the teaching we were listening to. The Word literally changed our lives even though we had read these same passages so many times before! When you have the right understanding and read the Word it comes alive and makes sense. Our lives were changed and the power to do that was right there the whole time. All we needed to do was change our thinking and believe. I am excited to share with you more about what I'm talking about.

And be not conformed to this world: but be ye transformed by the renewing of your mind, that ye may prove what is that good, and acceptable, and perfect, will of God. (Romans 12:2 KJV)

We see in Romans 12:2 that if we really want to be transformed it has to start on the inside and then move out. We can only be transformed by the renewing of our minds. We saw earlier in Romans 10:17 that, "faith comes by hearing and hearing by the Word," so getting the Word in our mind is critical.

Most people in life are conformed while thinking they are transformed. Being conformed means you are acting like everyone else. When you became a Christian you most likely took the belief system of whoever led you to Christ. I'm sure they were a great person and maybe even a close friend but did they have a revelation of the Word or did they just take on the belief system of whoever led them to Christ?

One of the hardest things to do sometimes is break traditions. We usually get our traditions from people who love us and lead us to the Lord whether it's a parent, friend, or maybe even a spouse. People that love you usually have the right intentions when they pass their belief system on to you.

This can be great or bad depending on their view of things. They can be 100% correct in one area of scripture but wrong in others. It doesn't matter how much you love or trust someone, including your pastor or myself; the Word of God is number one! It is great to have people in your life to help with understanding but always go back to scripture! God will speak to you, lead and guide you.

We see in Romans 12:2 that the reason to renew our mind is to be transformed and the reason to be transformed is to prove the will of God. God's will for us is great but sometimes we need to renew our minds before breakthrough can happen. Don't let what you don't know stop you from winning ever again. Now people may start to think about their traditions and say, "Wait, are you telling me that unless I change the way I think, breakthrough won't happen? Are you saying that I can stop the will of God?" To answer that I will always default to scripture and I pray this will help your eyes to see the Word and what it says in a new yet accurate way.

Dominion

I think if we are going to go through this together and dig into lots of scripture, the best place for us to start is at the beginning; in Genesis. In the beginning it says that God spoke everything into existence, created man, and gave him dominion. I have been really thinking about the word 'dominion' and its meaning. A lot of what we are going to be talking about will come from Genesis when God gave Adam dominion. Dictionary.com says this is the definition of dominion:

Do·min·ion

NOUN

1.the power or right of governing and controlling; sovereign authority.

2.rule; control; domination.

3.a territory, usually of considerable size, in which a single rulership holds sway.

4.lands or domains subject to sovereignty or control.

The Word says in Genesis;

Then God said, "Let Us make man in Our image, according to Our likeness; <u>let them have dominion</u> over the fish of the sea, over the birds of the air, and over the cattle, over all the earth and over every creeping thing that creeps on the earth." So God created man in His own image; in the image of God He created him; male and female He created them. Then God blessed them, and God said to them, "Be fruitful and multiply; fill the earth and subdue it; <u>have dominion</u> over the fish of the sea, over the birds of the air, and over every living thing that moves on the earth." (Genesis 1:26-28 NKJV)

You see at the very beginning, God not only created man but gave him a place to live and manage. God told Adam to name all the animals giving him authority over the animals, plants, and land. Everything God created on earth was given to Adam and Eve. We also see in Genesis that through disobedience, Satan stole Adam's dominion.

You ask, "what does that mean?" I get a lot of questions like, "if God is all loving why would He send people to hell?", or "if God is in control why do bad things happen to good people?" All of these can be answered from this account in Genesis about how man sinned. Satan was handed Adam's dominion through sin

(Adam's obedience to what the devil said instead of God).
There are so many scriptures to back this up.

-I will no longer talk much with you, <u>for the ruler of this world is coming</u>, and he has nothing in Me. (John 14:30 NKJV)

-Now is the judgment of this world; <u>now the ruler of this world</u> will be cast out. (John 12:31 NKJV)

-Then Jesus was led up by the Spirit into the wilderness to be tempted by the devil. And when He had fasted forty days and forty nights, afterward He was hungry. Now when the tempter came to Him, he said, "If You are the Son of God, command that these stones become bread." But He answered and said, "It is written, 'Man shall not live by bread alone, but by every word that proceeds from the mouth of God.'" Then the devil took Him up into the holy city, set Him on the pinnacle of the temple, and said to Him, "If You are the Son of God, throw Yourself down. For it is written: 'He shall give His angels charge over you,' and, 'In their hands they shall bear you up, Lest you dash your foot against a stone.'" Jesus said to him, "It is written again, 'You shall not tempt the LORD your God.'" Again, the devil took Him up on an exceedingly high mountain, and showed Him all the kingdoms of the world and their glory. And he said to Him, "<u>All these things I will give You</u> if You will fall down and worship me." Then Jesus said to him, "Away with you, Satan! For it is written, 'You shall worship the LORD your God, and Him only you shall serve.'" Then the devil left Him, and behold, angels came and ministered to Him. (Matthew 4:1-11 NKJV)

Look at when Jesus is tempted. Satan takes Him up on a high mountain and shows Him all the kingdoms of the world and their glory and says, "I will give them to you." Why didn't Jesus respond, "Those are not yours to give?" Why does it say Jesus was tempted? If you understand dominion and what was given to Adam and then what Adam gave away through sin, you will understand that Jesus came to take back what the devil had stole! He came to break the curse sin had over man and set you free.

The devil wants to destroy you. And just like in Matthew 4 when the devil tempted Jesus, the devil will tempt you as well. What was his trick with Jesus? He tried to get Jesus to doubt what God said. What was his trick in the garden in Genesis? He tricked Adam and Eve into doubting what God said. Think about this for a moment. In the garden Satan came up to Eve and said "Has God indeed said?" convincing her to doubt the Word of God with just a question. He is using the same old trick today that he's always used. He will plant a thought in your head and let you run with it so you will doubt what God said.

All fear, doubt, worry and anxiety will go away if we just believe the Word. God has promised to bless you and take care of you. He has made you in His image. He will never leave you and there is so much more! If the devil can get you to doubt what God says; he wins. If he can get you to doubt the Word and make you think you're all alone, broke, sick, going to die, ugly, worthless, that God could never use you and you will never be anything, then you will get down and depression will set in.

There is power in the Word but if Satan can get you to doubt the Word and what God said, you are in trouble. If Satan's plan was to destroy man, why didn't he just tempt Eve to kill Adam? If Adam was dead then wouldn't the devil have won? Mankind would have been over.

It all goes back to power in the Word of God. When God made Adam and Eve there were no 10 commandments or the law. What makes sin sin? Whatever God says is sin! So the devil could only go against what God had said. God hadn't yet said, "thou shalt not kill." He only said be fruitful, multiply, and do not eat of that one tree! The only thing the devil could do when going against the Word of God, was try and get them to eat of the tree.

There is power in the Word and power when you read it, not as just a good story book but as the Word of God. I've heard from many pastors over the years, "If you work the Word, the Word works." We know there is power in the Word and God gave us dominion so we have a place to start. Did God take back the dominion He gave to man? You might say yes, but look at what Romans says:

For the gifts and the calling of God are irrevocable. (Romans 11:29 NKJV)

This is talking about a Spiritual gift that God will not take back. God will not take any gifts away from you. You might also be thinking of Job when he said "the Lord gives and takes away!" We will cover this in Chapter 8 so hang in there. Look what it says in Numbers and Hebrews.

—God is not a man, that He should lie, Nor a son of man, that He should repent. Has He said, and will He not do? Or has He spoken, and will He not make it good? (Numbers 23:19 NKJV)

—Thus God, determining to show more abundantly to the heirs of promise the immutability of His counsel, confirmed it by an oath, that by two immutable things, in which it is impossible for God to lie, we might have strong consolation, who have fled for refuge to lay hold of the hope set before us. (Hebrews 6:17, 18 NKJV)

—Who being the brightness of His glory and the express image of His person, and upholding all things by the word of His power, when He had by Himself purged our sins, sat down at the right hand of the Majesty on high. (Hebrews 1:3 NKJV)

We see there in Hebrews 1:3 that not only is there power in the Word but He is upholding all things by the power of His Word. So, not only will God not take back from you but the world is held together by His Word. His Word is power and it is truth and God can not lie! I know the Word to be true and have seen it work over and over again in my life. There is power in the Word and when you put your faith in it, it will move mountains.

One of the big problems today is we don't know or think about the dominion that God gave to us. We think that God is this dictator in the sky that just controls everything. We hear all the time that He is a sovereign God.

The definition of sovereign in the dictionary is; all powerful or number one! "All controlling and nothing happens that wasn't my will," is not part of the definition. I do agree that God is all powerful but would disagree that God is all controlling. That would take away free will which is against His Word and what He has said.

We live in a fallen world and due to man's free will, God is not controlling everything. It is actually dangerous to teach that God is controlling everything. You raise questions like, "So then did God start all the wars?" and, "Is He ok with abortion?" and, "Did God take a loved one away from me with a disease?" The list goes on and on. This is a scary theology to base your worldview on not only because it goes against the Bible but because when we teach it people are inevitably going to get angry at God.

Think about this; how many times have you seen someone stand up in church on a Sunday and tell everyone that we serve a good God and then in the next breath tell Sister so-and-so they're so sorry her baby passed away but God's ways are higher than ours. Well which is it; is He a good God or did He just take their baby? If that is what a good God does then no wonder so many people are mad at Him. There are so many Christians that will just say something in an effort to try and comfort people when they don't have the answer. Although their heart is in the right place, it hurts people to just say things that go against the Bible just because we want to have an answer.

The thief does not come except to steal, and to kill, and to destroy.
I have come that they may have life, and that they may have it
more abundantly. John 10:10 NKJV

The Word is very clear. How can life and life more
abundantly be sickness or death when it clearly says the enemy
comes to do that? It is never a good thing when someone loses a
loved one and then we tell people that God took that person; it will
hurt people and make them angry at God for something the enemy
did.

I mentioned earlier that the question I get a lot is, "Why
would a loving God send someone to hell?" We need to realize a
few things in order to answer that question. First of all, the
question was asked incorrectly and usually asked with the
assumption of already knowing the answer. The real question is,
"Would an all loving God send someone to hell?", and the
answer is a big "NO!"

Now calm down a little. Let me explain. Do people go to
hell? The answer is "yes." Because Adam sinned, all of humanity
was on its way to hell already. It was because of an all loving God
who sent His Son that made it possible for us to not follow our sins
into hell.

For God so loved the world that He gave His only begotten Son,
that whoever believes in Him should not perish but have
everlasting life. For God did not send His Son into the world to
condemn the world, but that the world through Him might be
saved. "He who believes in Him is not condemned; but he who

does not believe is condemned already, because he has not believed in the name of the only begotten Son of God. John 3:16-18 NKJV

Hell was never created for you! In fact, heaven was not created for you either. Earth was created for you and was given to you but sin messed that up. In the Word it says that God will create a new heaven and a new earth and our present world will pass away. Think about that for a moment. Hell was created for the devil and all that follow him will follow him to hell. If God was controlling everything and there was no free will, no one would go to hell.

For this is good and acceptable in the sight of God our Savior, who desires all men to be saved and to come to the knowledge of the truth. For there is one God and one Mediator between God and men, the Man Christ Jesus, who gave Himself a ransom for all, to be testified in due time. (1 Timothy 2:3-6 NKJV).

He didn't just die for the sins of some but it says He died for the sins of the world! If you think about that it will blow your mind. There will be people in hell when their sins were already paid for. It's not sin that sends you to hell because Jesus took the sins of the world.

My little children, these things I write to you, so that you may not sin. And if anyone sins, we have an Advocate with the Father, Jesus Christ the righteous. And He Himself is the propitiation for our sins, and not for ours only but also for the whole world. (1 John 2:1, 2 NKJV)

So it is not God that sends us to hell but our personal decision not to accept Jesus Christ as Lord. It is not sin that sends you to hell but rejecting Jesus. Jesus is the only way to heaven and the Word is very clear about that.

Now is sin bad? Absolutely! Sin will destroy your life and keep you from everything that God has called you to do. It is a distraction and will mess you up. The devil will keep you in your sin, keep you thinking about sin, and thus you will continue to struggle with sin. This makes sin the center of everything instead of Jesus. But again, receiving Jesus is our choice. So this affirms that we have free will and live in a fallen world.

"I call heaven and earth as witnesses today against you, that I have set before you life and death, blessing and cursing; therefore choose life, that both you and your descendants may live;" Deuteronomy 30:19 NKJV

Another argument for dominion and God not controlling everything is Jesus. That may sound confusing at first but think about this for a moment. If God was like Thanos from Avengers and could just snap His fingers and change everything, why would He send Jesus? It seems to me that sending Jesus to be beaten, bruised, crucified, mocked, tortured and killed if there were any other options, would just be sick and wrong.

I believe God sent His only Son because there was no other way. He beat the devil at his own game. God gave Adam dominion which Satan stole through sin. God then came down in the flesh, as a man, and took back what the devil stole! God had to come down as Jesus Christ because He gave dominion to man and had to change things back as both fully God and fully man! If God had not given dominion to man why would He come down as a man and be crucified? He loved you enough to send His son as a man to be the sacrifice once and for all to cover all the sins of the world. Now just like the Israelites in Egypt putting the blood over the door post, you can have the blood of Jesus over your life so judgment will pass by you!

Our Right to Rule

God creating the world and then giving man dominion answers a lot of the questions we have today. We feel God is supposed to be doing everything when in fact He gave us dominion here and then empowered us with His Spirit. People are not getting the results they want to see and feel like they are on a hamster wheel in life. The fact that God needed to come down as fully God and fully man to change things is everything!

What is the number one way He works today? The Holy Spirit! Think about this for a moment. We believe in the trinity; God the Father, God the Son, and God the Holy Spirit. Jesus was able to change the world because He was fully God and fully man. Today we have the Holy Spirit in us and that is powerful. We are fully man with fully God inside us as the Holy Spirit.

People have no problem saying that the Holy Spirit is fully God and they have no problem saying the Holy Spirit is living in them. People have a hard time putting it all together so they walk around like they have nothing. It really does show us what we believe and how we think when we claim we are nothing.

The Word says *"I can do all things through Christ who strengthens me" (Philippians 4:13 NKJV)*. Who can do all things? I can do all things! How can I do all these things? Through Christ! It is not on our own. The fully man part that is you is not that impressive and although God has given you things you can do that are amazing, it's still in the natural. When you and the fully God part in you come together, then it becomes something special. It becomes supernatural. When you begin to understand who is on the inside of you and start to use your God given authority, being Holy Spirit led, there isn't anything you cannot do! Jesus promised the Holy Spirit would come and He is here!

Most assuredly, I say to you, he who believes in Me, the works that I do he will do also; and greater works than these he will do, because I go to My Father. And whatever you ask in My name, that I will do, that the Father may be glorified in the Son. If you ask anything in My name, I will do it. "If you love Me, keep My commandments. And I will pray the Father, and He will give you another Helper, that He may abide with you forever— the Spirit of truth, whom the world cannot receive, because it neither sees Him nor knows Him; but you know Him, for He dwells with you and will be in you. I will not leave you orphans; I will come to you. "A little while longer and the world will see Me no more, but you will see Me. Because I live, you will live also. At that day you will know that I am in My Father, and you in Me, and I in you. He who has My commandments and keeps them, it is he who loves Me. And he

who loves Me will be loved by My Father, and I will love him
and manifest Myself to him. (John 14:12-21 NKJV).

We are not only promised the Holy Spirit but that we will do greater things! Are we operating in the greater things yet? Jesus was the prototype for us all. We should look, act, and sound like Jesus. We shouldn't just say "What would Jesus do," but read what He did and do the same! Jesus was showing us how to move in power. He was both fully God and fully man. Just think what would happen if millions of Christians woke up and realized their dominion as a man with the Holy Spirit on the inside!

God has a plan and it involves you and I. We often beg God for revival instead of understanding he sent revival over 2,000 years ago as Jesus Christ. It's time the church stood up and was the rival. We have someone on the inside of us the world needs. So often, we are worried about being filled up with the Spirit when God said I've given you the Spirit without measure.

For He whom God has sent speaks the words of God, for God does
not give the Spirit by measure. John 3:34 NKJV.

So, we know that God does not give the Spirit with measure! God did not hold back on us in sending Jesus, He did not hold back on us in giving the Spirit and He will not hold back on us now! The Holy Spirit living on the inside of us is not just for us to get goose bumps at a meeting. The point was not just to be in us but to move through us. It's great to have Him on the inside but the point is to let Him out.

For our gospel did not come to you in word only, but <u>also in power, and in the Holy Spirit</u> and in much assurance, as you know what kind of men we were among you for your sake (1 Thessalonians 1:5 NKJV).

It was Paul that wrote Thessalonians and he was a man like you and me. He also didn't have that great of a start, certainly wasn't perfect, yet God used him for some amazing things! Paul started out killing Christians and ended up writing most of the New Testament! God is not looking for the qualified but He will qualify the ones that have enough faith to step out. We say that we are believers but are we really? Do we believe everything in His Word or do we just want to put a big "but" after everything? Again, do we let our experiences dictate the Word or do we let the Word transform our experiences?

CHAPTER 2

Rightly Divide Truth

Have you ever read 2 Timothy 2:15 and took note of how it talks about rightly dividing the word of truth?

Remind them of these things, charging them before the Lord not to strive about words to no profit, to the ruin of the hearers. Be diligent to present yourself approved to God, a worker who does not need to be ashamed, <u>rightly dividing the word of truth</u>. (2 Timothy 2:14-15 NKJV)

I was reading this and when I got to "rightly dividing the word of truth," I immediately thought, "what does that mean?" Most of the time you think about rightly dividing as dividing right and wrong or dividing good and evil but never dividing truth! The second thought was; if you can rightly divide truth then you must also be able to wrongly divide truth!

We also see in that scripture that there are "words to no profit." Instead of dividing the truth, we waste energy on things that don't matter. There are many things that we can argue about that do not bring life and I want to make sure that as the Body of Christ we only sharpen each other in the Word and let some things go. I believe that many Christians today are not rightly dividing truth and so they are left confused and frustrated in life. Let's talk a little bit about what it means to rightly divide the Word of Truth in this chapter.

After man sinned in the garden, the first thing that God did was kill an animal and make clothes for both Adam and Eve.

"Also for Adam and his wife the LORD God made tunics of skin, and clothed them." (Genesis 3:21 NKJV)

The reason this is so important is this is the first blood spilt! Wherever there is sin, blood must be shed. We see sacrifices all through scripture but this was the first blood shed and it was by God because of Adam and Eve's sin.

Fast forward to Cain and Abel and you see that God took Abel's offering but not Cain's.

"...Now Abel was a keeper of sheep, but Cain was a tiller of the ground. And in the process of time it came to pass that Cain brought an offering of the fruit of the ground to the LORD. Abel also brought of the firstborn of his flock and of their fat. And the LORD respected Abel and his offering, but He did not respect Cain and his offering. And Cain was very angry, and his countenance fell." (Genesis 4:2-5 NKJV).

God accepted Abel's offering because there was blood spilt which is what made Abel's offering different from Cain's. Instead of repentance this led to resentment and anger from Cain and ultimately the first murder.

From Adam and Eve all through the Old Testament, we see offerings had to be made and blood had to be spilt. When Moses took the Israelites from Egypt, we can see from the beginning that God just wanted His people to believe in Him and trust Him. When the Israelites told Moses they could do everything that God wanted, their inference was that they could do this on their own. The result was the Law being given.

The Law was never meant for us to fulfill! It was meant to show us that we need a savior. There are over 613 laws in the Old Testament. I can't even remember them all, let alone fulfill them. Then James says *"For whoever shall keep the whole law, and yet stumble in one point, he is guilty of all." (James 2:10 NKJV)*. Now if you fail at even one law and keep the rest, you are still guilty of them all! This makes verses like, *"for all have sinned and fall short of the glory of God," (Romans 3:23 NKJV)* come alive to us.

The law was never meant for us to fulfill but to point us to Jesus. It's crazy that people cannot fulfill the law but still put others under it every day. Just because we are not under the law today does not give us the right to go and sin though. I am saying we are now free from sin but not free to go sin. Sin will destroy your life. The message of grace has been misunderstood for a long time. Grace is not the cover up of our sin but is what empowers us to be free from sin. What I am saying is that we are free from the law now if we are in Christ Jesus.

There is therefore now no condemnation to those who are in Christ Jesus, who do not walk according to the flesh, but *according to the Spirit. For the law of the Spirit of life in <u>Christ</u> <u>Jesus has made me free from the law of sin and death</u>. For what the law could not do in that it was weak through the flesh, God did by sending His own Son in the likeness of sinful flesh, on account of sin: He condemned sin in the flesh, that the <u>righteous</u> <u>requirement of the law might be fulfilled in us who do not walk</u> <u>according to the flesh but according to the Spirit</u>. (Romans 8:1-4 NKJV)*

Romans lays it out plainly; we are now free in Christ Jesus. There will always be those people who want to go back under the law, and put it all back on you. They say, "Yes, but it says for those who do not walk according to the flesh." What they are doing is trying to make it all about you again and your performance and if you mess up now there is condemnation again.

What they are really saying is the blood of Jesus–which God says is strong enough to take all the sins of the world all at one time–washes right off if you screw up one time. Now we are comparing the blood of Jesus to that of a goat or sheep back under the law. We need to read all of Romans 8 so we can rightly divide Truth. You are not rightly dividing the Word when you read a line instead of the verse, chapter, book or whole Bible. Romans is very clear what it is talking about if you keep reading.

But you are not in the flesh but in the Spirit, if indeed the Spirit of God dwells in you. Now if anyone does not have the Spirit of Christ, he is not His. (Romans 8:9 NKJV)

All it takes is just a little more reading and it spells out what walking in the Spirit is. If we have accepted Jesus we are no longer in the flesh but now in the Spirit because He dwells in us. Remember, there is now no condemnation for those who are walking in the Spirit and we are walking in the Spirit if we have accepted Christ. We want to make it about behavior but God makes it about Jesus. Old Covenant (the Law) was all about what we could do to be right. The New Covenant (Blood of Jesus) is all about what He did. The Law was not bad at all; in fact it was perfect. The problem was we couldn't do it; so again, we need to rely on Jesus. Jesus was not coming to get rid of the Law but fulfill it!

For as many as are of the works of the law are under the curse; for it is written, "Cursed is everyone who does not continue in all things which are written in the book of the law, to do them." But that no one is justified by the law in the sight of God is evident, for "the just shall live by faith." Yet the law is not of faith, but "the man who does them shall live by them." <u>*Christ has redeemed us from the curse of the law, having become a curse for us*</u> *(for it is written, "Cursed is everyone who hangs on a tree"), that the blessing of Abraham might come upon the Gentiles in Christ Jesus, that we might receive the promise of the Spirit through faith. (Galatians 3:10-14 NKJV)*

The Spirit Himself bears witness with our spirit that we are children of God, and if children, then heirs—heirs of God and joint heirs with Christ, if indeed we suffer with Him, that we may also be glorified together. (Romans 8:16, 17 NKJV)

The law is all about you and your actions. The New
Covenant is all about Jesus and what He did for you. Think about
this for a minute. Not everything that Jesus did is for us to do. We
often hear people say "be like Jesus" and in most cases, yes, that's
true. There are some things though, that when looking at the life of
Jesus are not for us to do. Jesus came to do what we couldn't do.
Jesus came and fulfilled the law. He didn't get rid of it, He finished
it. So now, you and I do not have to do what was already done.
Now we just need to accept Jesus and the New Covenant. Again, I
want to be clear, this does not mean we do whatever we want in
life. Grace is the key to live sin free and walk holy. When
immature Christians hear grace, they always think, "does this mean
that I can do what I want?" Paul answered this with, "God forbid,
certainly not!" So rightly dividing the Truth (Word of God) means
recognizing what covenant you are under.

Old Covenant, New Covenant

*Behold, the days are coming, says the LORD, when I will
make a new covenant with the house of Israel and with the house
of Judah— not according to the covenant that I made with their
fathers in the day that I took them by the hand to lead them out of
the land of Egypt, My covenant which they broke, though I was a
husband to them, says the LORD. But this is the covenant that I
will make with the house of Israel after those days, says the LORD:
I will put My law in their minds, and write it on their hearts; and I
will be their God, and they shall be My people. No more shall
every man teach his neighbor, and every man his brother, saying,
'Know the LORD,' for they all shall know Me, from the least of
them to the greatest of them, says the LORD. For I will forgive*

their iniquity, and their <u>sin I will remember no more</u>.
(Jeremiah 31:31-34 NKJV)

Now is the season of the New Covenant; He will be our God and we will be His people. With the law, one always had to bring a sacrifice and it was only good for a season. With the New Covenant, Jesus became the sacrifice once for all!

And the Word became flesh and dwelt among us, and we beheld His glory, the glory as of the only begotten of the Father, full of grace and truth. John bore witness of Him and cried out, saying, "This was He of whom I said, 'He who comes after me is preferred before me, for He was before me.'" And of His fullness we have all received, and grace for grace. <u>For the law was given through Moses</u>, but <u>grace and truth came through Jesus Christ</u>. (John 1:14-17 NKJV)

You see, rightly dividing Truth is really dividing the two covenants! You can not be living under one covenant but still trying to fulfill the other. I have heard different speakers not fully understand the two and so they preach about the blood of Jesus and then in the next breath talk about how if you are in sin God is going to get you. All sins were covered and paid for on the cross over 2,000 years ago! Now, it's not about sin but about whether you have Jesus. The new covenant is all about Jesus and what He did. Even if we could fulfill the law it still wouldn't have been enough.

"Jesus said to him, 'I am the way, the truth, and the life. No one comes to the Father except through Me.'" (John 14:6 NKJV)

So, why don't we just do whatever we want if all sin was paid for? The reason is that God still hates sin and it's not of Him. When we sin it opens us up for the devil to come in and try to destroy us. The closer you get to God, the less you should want anything to do with sin. The Holy Spirit living on the inside of you should be speaking to you every day. You will feel so bad when you do something wrong that it will eat at you. We were not designed to sin and it goes against who we were created to be. We are created in the image of God and sin is not in His character.

You might be thinking, "what does all of this have to do with healing?" This is most people's hang-up on getting their breakthrough. When you think you have to do something to get God to do something, you go back under the law. "Rightly dividing" is the realization that Jesus paid it all and we are no longer under the law. You have to divide healing stories in the Bible and ask what covenant it is under.

Even stories of Jesus were still under the Old Covenant because He came to fulfill the law. The New Covenant didn't start until after Jesus died and rose again. Do you remember the story of the man sitting at the pool of Bethesda? He was sitting around waiting for the stirring of the water and Jesus came and did something new. Look at the statement Jesus told him, "go and sin no more or something worse will happen."

When Jesus saw him lying there, and knew that he already had been in that condition a long time, He said to him, "Do you want to be made well?" The sick man answered Him, "Sir, I have no man to put me into the pool when the water is stirred up; but while I am coming, another steps down before me." Jesus said to him, "Rise, take up your bed and walk." And immediately the man was made well, took up his bed, and walked. And that day was the Sabbath. The Jews therefore said to him who was cured, "It is the Sabbath; it is not lawful for you to carry your bed." He answered them, "He who made me well said to me, 'Take up your bed and walk.' " Then they asked him, "Who is the Man who said to you, 'Take up your bed and walk?'" But the one who was healed did not know who it was, for Jesus had withdrawn, a multitude being in that place. Afterward Jesus found him in the temple, and said to him, "See, you have been made well. Sin no more, lest a worse thing come upon you." (John 5:6-14 NKJV)

I've seen many Christians make a doctrine out of that statement alone. They state that if you are sick then there is sin in your life. I've heard from many people that if you sin or mess up then sickness can come on you. That's just not the case! There may be natural consequences of our behavior but it is not a punishment from God. People misunderstand this statement from Jesus, but you have to realize that sickness is not of God and God doesn't put sickness on anyone because of sin.

We need to rightly divide here and see that Jesus was 100% correct for saying this to the man because they were still under the law at that time. Jesus was warning him not to sin "unless something worse happen," because at that time, it was all about us and what we did. The law was always about if we do bad things then bad will happen but if you do good things then good will happen. If you read through Deuteronomy 28, you can see both the blessing and the curses and guess what, sickness was always and will always be under the curse! It was never from God. He sent Jesus to redeem us from the curse, not use the curse to teach us something.

Dividing the Word of Truth is Elijah calling down fire (Old Covenant) and Jesus rebuking his disciples for wanting to call down fire (New Covenant). In Deuteronomy 28 when you did things wrong and didn't trust God then bad things happened. There was also a blessing though in Deuteronomy 28.

"Now it shall come to pass, if you diligently obey the voice of the LORD your God, to observe carefully all His commandments which I command you today, that the LORD your God will set you high above all nations of the earth. And all these blessings shall come upon you and overtake you, because you obey the voice of the LORD your God:" (Deuteronomy 28:1-2 NKJV)

It doesn't say we were blessed for only doing "good" but we had to obey ALL His commandments. Now remember, there are 613 commandments and if you were guilty of one you were guilty of them all! So who was blessed then if you had to fulfill the law to be blessed? You guessed it–no one saw the blessing like they should have. Praise God that Jesus fulfilled the law and now if we are in Christ Jesus and He is in us, then we also have fulfilled the law and the requirements for the blessing. Healing is part of that blessing! Abraham did see the blessing but remember he wasn't under the law either! He believed God and it was accounted to him as righteousness. The law never came until Moses.

Now read Deuteronomy 28 while rightly dividing Truth and we see that we have fulfilled the law in Jesus and we can take this scripture as our promise from God! It's only because of Jesus and what Jesus did that makes this all possible. There is nothing we could do to earn this free gift we get from just believing.

"Now it shall come to pass, if you diligently obey the voice of the LORD your God, to observe carefully all His commandments which I command you today, that the LORD your God will set you high above all nations of the earth. And all these blessings shall come upon you and overtake you, because you obey the voice of the LORD your God: "Blessed shall you be in the city, and blessed shall you be in the country. "Blessed shall be the fruit of your body, the produce of your ground and the increase of your herds, the increase of your cattle and the offspring of your flocks. "Blessed shall be your basket and your kneading bowl. "Blessed shall you be when you come in, and blessed shall you be when you go out. "The LORD will cause your enemies who rise against you to be defeated before your face; they shall come out against you one way and flee before you seven ways. "The LORD will command the blessing on you in your storehouses and in all to which you set your hand, and He will bless you in the land which the LORD your God is giving you. "The LORD will establish you as a holy people to Himself, just as He has sworn to you, if you keep the commandments of the LORD your God and walk in His ways. Then all peoples of the earth shall see that you are called by the name of the LORD, and they shall be afraid of you. And the

LORD will grant you plenty of goods, in the fruit of your body, in the increase of your livestock, and in the produce of your ground, in the land of which the LORD swore to your fathers to give you. The LORD will open to you His good treasure, the heavens, to give the rain to your land in its season, and to bless all the work of your hand. You shall lend to many nations, but you shall not borrow. And the LORD will make you the head and not the tail; you shall be above only, and not be beneath, if you heed the commandments of the LORD your God, which I command you today, and are careful to observe them. So you shall not turn aside from any of the words which I command you this day, to the right or the left, to go after other gods to serve them." (Deuteronomy 28:1-14 NKJV)

We see Jesus came to set us free from the law and redeem what the devil stole in the garden. We were in a perfect place just meant to live, thrive and spend time with God until sin entered in. Read Galatians 3:12-14.

"Yet the law is not of faith, but "the man who does them shall live by them." <u>Christ has redeemed us from the curse of the law</u>, having become a curse for us (for it is written, "Cursed is everyone who hangs on a tree"), <u>that the blessing of Abraham might come upon the Gentiles in Christ Jesus</u>, that we might receive the promise of the Spirit through faith." (Galatians 3:12-14 NKJV)

We see Jesus delivered us from the curse in Deuteronomy 28 so that the blessing could come, not just on the Jews, but the Gentiles as well. That means the blessings are for you and me today because of Jesus and His Blood. God made a covenant with Abraham and through Jesus we can all take part in His blood covenant.

A Blood Covenant

Have you ever researched blood covenants? I taught a college class on blood covenant and when I started to research it I was astonished by everything that Jesus did for us and the covenant He made with His people. Understanding this blood covenant better is crucial to accessing the healing breakthrough you need.

When we rightly divide Truth we can see that we don't just have a new covenant but that Jesus is the new covenant and all things in Jesus are good. With this blood covenant understanding we have all the benefits of what Jesus did on the cross. There are many reasons for a blood covenant and also many effects of a blood covenant but as you look at them you can see that Jesus didn't do just one, He did them all!

-Reasons for blood covenant
1. Tribal alliance
2. Business partnership
3. Devoted love
-Effects of the blood covenant
1. Debts and possessions are shared
2. All the benefits, talents, assets, liabilities, and debts of the first person are owned and shared equally by the second person and all the debts, assets, liabilities and

talents of the second person are equally shared by the first person

3. It includes everything you are, everything you own, and everything you owe

4. The covenant is so binding that the two would become one

a. They would cease to exist as individuals and only exist in relation to the covenant

b. We are not to operate apart from our covenant with God and He does not operate apart from His covenant with us

Looking at this you can see that with this covenant the two are now one. This is a game changer for Christians to realize. In early history different tribes would cut their hands and either shake or drip the blood in a cup and drink it. This was saying that they had an alliance together and if one tribe goes to war the other will join. This is the same with God with the shedding of blood and the blood of Jesus now in your life. When you go into battle God will be going into battle with you. You no longer are fighting alone! All of your problems are now His problems and all His benefits are now yours!

You see that in a marriage; the two become one! This is the same with God. It's important to realize that. When you read through scriptures and He is talking about the bride of Christ, He is saying that the two are one. In both a marriage and business covenant, the two are one entity now and all debt and assets are joint owned! There is so much that Jesus did on the cross and we don't want to miss even one of the benefits of the cross!

Bless and affectionately praise the LORD, O my soul,

And do not forget any of His benefits; (Psalms 103:2 AMP)

After a blood covenant is made there are several things that take place as an outward seal of what was done. Whether its tribes exchanging gifts, in a marriage the changing of names, or sometimes just the cutting/blood that took place; Jesus did all of this for us! We see because of His blood shed for us, we now have a new name and He also left us gifts. He sealed the deal in so many ways so we should never question what He did for us; yet people do.

People do not understand covenant because we view God through our lens instead of trying to view ourselves through God's lens. Back in the day they would cut themselves as a promise. In the old west, instead of the cutting, they would spit in their hand as a covenant. Today we have long contracts with lots of lawyers involved in case someone goes against their word. We can't view God's covenant through the lens of man's imperfections. God changed our name and now calls us son. Jesus shed His blood and He left us (gifts) the Holy Spirit!

Nevertheless I tell you the truth. It is to your advantage that I go away; for if I do not go away, the Helper will not come to you; but if I depart, I will send Him to you. And when He has come, He will convict the world of sin, and of righteousness, and of judgment: of sin, because they do not believe in Me; of righteousness, because I go to My Father and you see Me no more; of judgment, because the ruler of this world is judged. "I still have

*many things to say to you, but you cannot bear them now.
However, when He, the Spirit of truth, has come, He will guide you
into all truth; for He will not speak on His own authority, but
whatever He hears He will speak; and He will tell you things to
come. He will glorify Me, for He will take of what is Mine and
declare it to you. All things that the Father has are Mine.
Therefore I said that He will take of Mine and declare it to you.
(John_16:7-15 NKJV)*

This is such a powerful passage packed with
breakthrough truth for those who will see it! Jesus is literally
saying that everything that the Father has is His and everything
that He has is now ours through the Holy Spirit! This sounds like
the two-become-one covenant. We often think that the Holy Spirit
is here to convict us and make us feel bad all the time. This is
because we are not rightly dividing the Truth. If we look in John
16 we see that the Holy Spirit will do three things. The Holy Spirit
will convict the world of sin, He will convict of righteousness, and
He will bring Judgment.

*And when He is come, He will reprove the world of sin,
and of righteousness, and of judgment: of sin, because they
believe not on me; of righteousness, because I go to my Father,
and ye see me no more; of judgment, because the prince of this
world is judged. (John 16:8-11 KJV)*

Let's look at it closely. It says convict the world of sin
(because they haven't believed me), of righteousness (this is the
Christians, because I go to my Father) and judge (the prince of this

world or the Devil). This is what is crazy, He needs to convict Christians not of sin but of our righteousness.

How often do we need to be convicted that we are in Christ? We let the devil get in our ear and tell us we are nothing and that we have nothing when it is the exact opposite. We have a blood covenant and what Jesus did for us was not cheap. He paid a high price for our freedom, so let's walk in it.

Shalom

Let's not forget all His benefits because we haven't been rightly dividing the Truth. We think we are still under the Old Covenant when Jesus put us under a new one in Him. It will be very hard to ever receive a healing if you don't know which covenant you are under. You will always be trying to get God to do something He already did over 2,000 years ago. Look at John 14:27.

Peace I leave with you, My peace I give to you; not as the world gives do I give to you. Let not your heart be troubled, neither let it be afraid. (John 14:27 NKJV)

We sometimes think that peace is sitting by a beach somewhere but that is not at all what Jesus is talking about here. That word peace was originally the word Shalom and has a much bigger meaning than we think.

Shalom (Hebrew: שָׁלוֹם shalom; also spelled as sholom, sholem, sholoim, shulem) is a Hebrew word meaning

peace, harmony, wholeness, completeness, prosperity, welfare and tranquility.

When Jesus was about to be crucified, this is what He told His disciples. How could He tell them not to let their heart be troubled right before His horrific death? How does anyone say "let not your heart be troubled" in such a troubling situation? If we understand the meaning of shalom we can then understand why Jesus could say this.

Look at the verse again. It isn't just peace that Jesus was leaving but peace, harmony, wholeness, completeness, prosperity, welfare and tranquility all in one! Now look at what He says; He isn't just leaving Shalom for us but HIS Shalom that is His peace, harmony, wholeness, completeness, prosperity, welfare and tranquility all in one. We have Jesus's everything. He held back nothing from us! We can see after we rightly divide and realize what covenant we are under we can receive every gift from him and that includes healing.

Shalom written out in Hebrew is 4 words put together! Yes, when they are together they do mean peace, harmony, wholeness, completeness, prosperity, welfare and tranquility all in one, but there is even more. The 4 words of Shalom in the Hebrew are Chaos, Attached, Authority and Destroy.

This might not look like much until we realize Hebrew reads from right to left! Now when we look at it Shalom is literally "to destroy the authority attached to chaos." To destroy the works of the devil! Not only do we have authority to do this but remember Jesus said My Shalom I leave you. We have Jesus' authority to destroy the works of the devil! We can destroy the chaos in our life!

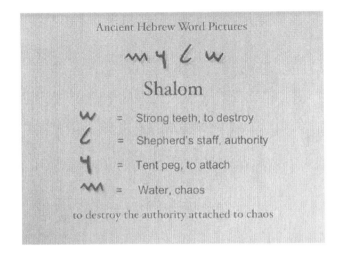

Ancient Hebrew Word Pictures

Shalom

W = Strong teeth, to destroy

ℓ = Shepherd's staff, authority

Ч = Tent peg, to attach

ᴍ = Water, chaos

to destroy the authority attached to chaos

CHAPTER 3

Is It God's Will To Heal?

In this chapter I want to break down this age-old question, "Is it God's will for you to be healed?" This may seem like a strange question for some and others will say, "How can you know the will of God?" If you realize from chapter two you have a blood covenant, you should also realize that it's not only God's will for you to be healed but He already paid for it.

How many times have you been to a Sunday service and heard a person praying over someone and saying the phrase "God if it's your will" or "In your timing oh Lord." It happens every day and we don't even realize what we are doing as Christians. We always pray as if it has nothing to do with us and all to do with God. This can be a scary statement but let me assure you that you can do nothing without Him. We hear people say all the time that we are nothing without Christ. That is true and I believe it to be, but then we must also believe that we are everything with Christ.

I can do all things through Christ which strengtheneth me. (Philippians 4:13 KJV)

Then Peter said, " Silver and gold have I none; but such as I have give I thee: In the name of Jesus Christ of Nazareth rise up and walk." (Acts 3:6 KJV)

We didn't think it crazy when Peter said, "such as I have give I you", but if someone said that today we would jump all over them and say, "No you don't have anything, it's all about God." We forget the blood covenant and that the two became one and now we get to walk around with our head held high as if God wants to change the world through us, because He does! He wants us to realize that it is all about Him living in us and moving through us. If we sit around and wait on God to do something He already did 2,000 years ago we will wait a long time. I've said it many times before that you can never get God to do something He has already done and you can never get God to do something He commanded you to do.

Watch Your Prayers

I was in Texas one Sunday right after one of our Kingdom Youth Conference and the pastor said, "we are going to turn and pray with those around us at this time". So, I looked around for one of the pastors that I knew needed a healing miracle and went over to him to start praying. As we started to pray, a man came over from the congregation and began praying very loudly, crying, and saying, "Lord, if it's your will, please find it in your great sovereignty to heal our brother in your perfect timing." I just felt sick in my stomach and really didn't like that approach to God our Father. After we were done, I pulled the young pastor aside and said, "Realize today that it is God's will for this healing miracle." He turned, looked at me and asked, "How can we know it's His will right now and it's His timing?" I smiled and said, "Because He paid for it on the cross over 2,000 years ago already!" He looked at me with a big smile and said, "Thank you so much."

When that man was praying, something just didn't feel right on the inside. Now I'm not saying the man's intentions were bad at all. He was just doing what he was taught to do by religion and tradition. We need to realize that although there are some good things with tradition and religion, those things never got anyone breakthrough. Breakthrough comes with a relationship with the Father! You don't see Peter coming up to the man and saying, "Silver and gold have I none but if it's God's will you can be healed." We didn't see him laying hands on the man and start crying because he felt bad. Peter understood what was given to Him and freely gave!

Another time, I was in Minnesota and the pastor stopped the services and said, "This brother in the back has cancer and we all need to pray for a miracle right now." I got excited because that is what church is about or should be. We need to be standing with each other in times of need. People need to know they are not going through something alone. It is not only God who is with them to fight their battles but also a body of believers!

So, the pastor starts to pray and says something along the lines of, "Lord, we know you are the healer, please be with the family in this time of need and bring peace. Please be with the doctors and give them wisdom. Please be the hope where there is no hope." When he was done praying, I thought, if God answers 100% of what he said, that man will still die of cancer.

It was a moment of realization for me. We need to think before we pray because there is power in prayer. Sometimes we don't know what to say so we just say lots of words hoping we don't say something wrong. Or we get afraid and think "what if it doesn't happen", thus limiting the power behind our prayer. The sad part of this story is that they prayed for him and that man still died of cancer.

It's easy to look at a scenario like that and think it just wasn't God's timing or God must have needed him in heaven. Those are some of the most common and worst things to ever say. First, God doesn't need you in heaven for anything. He created the universe with His voice. I think He will be alright with you staying on earth. In fact, where He needs you is on earth to tell others about Him! Even Paul said:

For I am hard-pressed between the two, having a desire to depart and be with Christ, which is far better. Nevertheless to remain in the flesh is more needful for you. And being confident of this, I know that I shall remain and continue with you all for your progress and joy of faith, that your rejoicing for me may be more abundant in Jesus Christ by my coming to you again. (Philippians 1:23-26 NKJV)

We can not view God through our experiences but must view God through the Word to change our experiences! Sometimes we think that because we had something bad happen to us in a fallen world that God must be a certain way. But we must always go back to what the Word says. So, how do we know that healing is the will of God? Because the Word tells us repeatedly it is! This does not mean that you will experience a healing every time, this just means that healing is the will of God! Let's look at some scripture and see if it's even possible to know the will of God.

And do not be conformed to this world, but be transformed by the renewing of your mind, <u>that you may prove what is that good and acceptable and perfect will of God.</u> (Romans 12:2 NKJV)

You see in Romans 12:2 that it is so important to renew your mind to the Word of God. If you start finding yourself believing anything that goes against the Word, you need to go back and renew it. This is a daily thing and is so important. Scripture says, if you don't do this you will be conformed to the world. We see this all this time when Christians start sounding like the mainstream media on their stances on certain things.

Look at the very last line of Romans 12:2. It clearly states, "...that you may prove what is the good and acceptable and perfect will of God." It would not say this if it was impossible to even know the will of God. If you are supposed to renew your mind to prove the will of God then it must be possible to know it! Also, Ephesians 5:17 tells us that we are supposed to understand the will of the Lord. It even goes as far as to say that it is unwise to not know the will of the Lord!

Therefore do not be unwise, but understand what the will of the Lord is. (Ephesians 5:17 NKJV)

For I know the plans and thoughts that I have for you,' says the LORD, 'plans for peace and well-being and not for disaster, to give you a future and a hope. (Jeremiah 29:11 AMP)

We see in Jeremiah that not only does God have plans for us (His will) but they are good plans! Plans for well-being. I'm not sure if you have ever been sick before but that really does go against our well-being. Remember that sickness was always under the curse. Even when the law was around it was never part of the blessing but always part of the curse. That is the same curse that we have been redeemed from. That is the same curse that Jesus became in order to free us. The same curse that we now have a blood covenant against. God's will is always good; giving us a future, hope, and well-being. It's all wrapped up into that Shalom we talked about.

Heaven On Earth

So, we see that we can know what the will of God is and we see that it is good. Even in the Lord's prayer He says:

Pray, then, in this way: 'Our Father, who is in heaven, Hallowed be Your name. Your kingdom come, Your will be done On earth as it is in heaven.' (Matthew 6:9-10 AMP)

It says, "Your Kingdom come, Your will be done." Where? "On earth as it is in heaven." This is another game changer. Why? Because, there are so many people that talk about being healed one way or another. It will either be here or in heaven. This just leaves a back door open in case a miracle doesn't happen. Matthew says you can pray that God's will be done on earth just the same as it is in heaven. I do not see sickness in heaven, I do not see lack in heaven, I do not see torment in heaven! We need to set people free from that on earth just as it is in heaven!

I think the best way to know the will of God is to know the character of God. If we can know the character of God we can know His will. How many of you have good friends that would stick up for you if they heard some crazy rumor about you. Do you have the kind of friends that would say, "No that's not true because I know them!".

This is how we should be with our God. We should know Him to the point that when someone says God took their child or God is teaching them something through suffering, we can look at them and say, "That's not my God.". We can say, "I know Him and that's not in His character."

I know some people right now have some Old Testament stories going through their heads and that is why we discussed "rightly dividing the truth" back in chapter two. I am also going to go into more detail about some of them later, such as Job, Paul and his thorn-in-the-flesh, and so much more. So put a pin in those questions for right now and follow me first on the will of God before we dive into all that.

I think the best way to know the character of God would be to look at Jesus. If we can see the character of Jesus, we can see the character of God because they are one. We believe that Jesus was both fully God and fully man but when we see something Jesus did it is sometimes hard to look at God the same.

"If you had [really] known Me, you would also have known My Father. <u>From now on you know Him, and have seen Him.</u>" Philip said to Him, "Lord, show us the Father and then we will be satisfied." Jesus said to him, "Have I been with you for so long a time, and you do not know Me yet, Philip, nor recognize clearly who I am? <u>Anyone who has seen Me has seen the Father.</u> How can you say, 'Show us the Father?' <u>Do you not believe that I am in the Father, and the Father is in Me?</u> The words I say to you I do not say on My own initiative or authority, <u>but the Father, abiding continually in Me</u>, does His works [His attesting miracles and acts of power]. <u>Believe Me that I am in the Father and the Father is in Me</u>; otherwise <u>believe [Me] because of the [very] works themselves</u> [which you have witnessed]. I assure you and most solemnly say to you, <u>anyone who believes in Me [as Savior] will also do the things that I do; and he will do even greater things than these</u> [in extent and outreach], because I am going to the Father. And I will do whatever you ask in My name [as My representative], <u>this I will do, so that the Father may be glorified and celebrated in the Son.</u> If you ask Me anything in My name [as My representative], I will do it. If you [really] love Me, you will keep and obey My commandments." (John 14:7-15 AMP)

This passage is very clear; if you have seen Jesus, you have seen the Father. The two are one. Jesus does nothing on His own but only what the Father is doing. It also ends with the power that we have because of the blood covenant and what Jesus did. Jesus also says that you will do greater things than these! So Jesus heals blind eyes, casts out demons, brings people back from the dead, walks on water and so much more, and then follows it up by saying, "greater things will you do in My name." You see, it is not selfish to think like this, like many have taught. In fact, it is the exact opposite. If we do not think like this, it is selfish because Jesus paid a high price for us to have the Holy Spirit and power.

For God knew his people in advance, and he chose them to become like his Son, so that his <u>Son would be the firstborn among many brothers and sisters</u>. (Romans 8:29 NLT)

Jesus was the firstborn of many. This means that He was the prototype for what we should all look like. He was the perfect model and we should all strive to be like Him. He did not just come to heal but show us how to heal. His job was to reverse the curse and show us how to take back our dominion again. We have a job to do as Chrsitians and sometimes we want to just sit back and put it all on God saying, "if it be His will." This makes for lazy Christians with weak prayers because we think it doesn't really matter and God will do what God will do.

The life of Jesus should be examined carefully on how He prayed and how He did everything. We can see the will of God through the life of Jesus so let's always be looking at Jesus. I want my prayers to sound like His prayers and I want my results to look like His results. If we look today at how we pray, it looks nothing like how Jesus prayed or His disciples. Not one of them ever begged God for something that He already did.

"Heal the sick, raise the dead, cure those with leprosy, and cast out demons. Give as freely as you have received!" (Matthew 10:8 NLT)

Matthew says it clearly that we need to give just as we have received. This is a commandment not a suggestion. It isn't about checking in to see if it's the will of God when He commanded us to do it. It does not say pray for healing for the sick. It says heal the sick. It does not say beg me to raise the dead. It says raise the dead. These are commandments from God because He already paid for it. This is about God working through us; Him putting His Holy Spirit on the inside of us so we can get something done. It is not our power but His that does the miracle but He is living inside us. It would be silly to call up the power company and tell them to turn on your lights when your light switch is off. They would tell you to just flip the switch! It's not your power running the house. The power company provided it but you need to flip the switch.

Looking at the life of Jesus we see the will of God in that Jesus never told anyone "no" when they asked for healing. He never said it is not the right time. In fact, most places He went He healed them all. This is important because we see people flocking to Jesus because He didn't turn people away. If Jesus and God are one then we can not say that it is not God's will for someone to be healed when Jesus and God are the same. Here are some of the scripture that show that Jesus healed everyone when He went places.

*That evening many demon-possessed people were brought to
Jesus. He cast out the evil spirits with a simple command, and <u>he
healed all the sick</u>. (Matthew 8:16 NLT)*

*Jesus saw the huge crowd as he stepped from the boat, and he had
compassion on them and <u>healed their sick</u>. (Matthew 14:14 NLT)*

*But Jesus knew what they were planning. So he left that area,
and many people followed <u>him. He healed all the sick among</u>
them. (Matthew 12:15 NLT)*

*Wherever he went—in villages, cities, or the countryside—they
brought the sick out to the marketplaces. They begged him to let
the sick touch at least the fringe of his robe, and <u>all who
</u>touched <u>him were healed</u>. (Mark 6:56 NLT)*

*He had healed many people that day, so <u>all the sick people
eagerly pushed forward to touch him</u>. (Mark 3:10 NLT)*

*As the sun went down that evening, people throughout the village
brought sick family members to Jesus. <u>No matter what their
diseases were, the touch of his hand healed every one</u>. (Luke
4:40 NLT)*

*Everyone tried to touch him, because healing power
went out from him, and <u>he healed everyone</u>. (Luke 6:19 NLT)*

*But the crowds found out where he was going, and
they followed him. He welcomed them and taught them about the*

Kingdom of God, and he healed those who were sick. (Luke 9:11 NLT)

Why is there so much scripture that says He healed them all? Because it is God's will!

Then Jesus answered and said to them, "Most assuredly, I say to you, the Son can do nothing of Himself, but what He sees the Father do; for whatever He does, the Son also does in like manner." (John 5:19 NKJV)

It is very easy to go through scripture and see that Jesus and God are one. When we see that Jesus is the Healer this also means God is the Healer. Throughout the gospels we see that Jesus never turned anyone away and had a heart for people. The **one time** in scripture where it says He "could not" do many works was because of **their** unbelief. It was about their unbelief, not that He didn't want to heal but because they were not ready to believe yet.

You Have To Do It

So if it's obvious throughout scripture that it's God's will to heal and if Jesus healed them all, then why is everyone not healed today? We need to think about where the problem comes from? The only two possibilities are; either God is doing something wrong or we are?

We are going to go through this in detail. I just want to say, when people get a revelation of the Word and healing, the Devil will bring condemnation that you are not good enough and you are praying wrong. The Holy Spirit brings conviction not condemnation.

The devil will want to take the right revelation and put it under the law again, making it all about you. Did I pray right, did I say the right things, do I have enough faith or maybe I doubted so now it's not going to happen. We need to realize that we have a job to do and we can only do it because of what Jesus did and His power within us. Without Him we are nothing but with Him the sky's the limits.

God is only limited by what you believe. We need to renew our mind to PROVE the perfect will of God (Romans 12:2). He isn't trying to just get the Holy Spirit to you so you can have all the special feels that you see in some churches. God isn't just trying to get the Holy Spirit **to** you but **through** you. Remember, it's God that empowers you and the moment you start to think it's about you, you will get into weirdness. Before Jesus ascended into heaven, He empowered His disciples.

One day Jesus called together his twelve disciples and gave them power and authority to cast out all demons and to heal all diseases. Then he sent them out to tell everyone about the Kingdom of God and to heal the sick. (Luke 9:1-2 NLT)

And when He had called His twelve disciples to Him, He gave them power over unclean spirits, to cast them out, and to heal all kinds of sickness and all kinds of disease. (Matthew 10:1 NKJV)

Jesus gave them the power! Go back and read it again! We walk around like we don't have anything when we have everything. We think we have been sitting around waiting on God when He has been waiting on us. He gave us the power and yet we keep asking for it. How can we ask God for something He already gave to us and how can we get God to do something He commanded us to do.

God is number one and all powerful but remember from chapter one that doesn't mean all controlling. He set us up for the win and it's time to know what we have.

Think of it like this. I bought a house, so it is my house and I own it. I give my daughter a room and tell her to keep it clean. I am not going to go in and clean it for her. She is old enough to do what I ask with what I've given her. Now, I can remind her of what I said and reiterate that I gave her the room to take care of but if I go in and do what I asked her to do, I would be doing her a disservice. I know it is not the exact concept with God but you can see that He commanded us to go out and empowered us to do so. He isn't just saying go do but saying go do because I'm living in you!

God didn't just snap His fingers to defeat the devil, He sent Jesus down as a man and beat the Devil at his own game and then He sent the Holy Spirit to live inside us. We need to realize that God putting the Holy Spirit in us is not without purpose but so that we have the power to continue what Jesus started.

I hope this is all starting to click so you can receive more scripture and it will open up and make more sense. God giving man dominion required God to come down as a man to take back what the devil stole. Jesus defeated the devil as a man and then said it is better for me to go so the Holy Spirit can come. Why? Now Jesus can be inside us and we can do greater things. There is a lot to do on this earth and that's why He is the first among many brethren. He wanted to be in all Christians so we can get so much more done. "Thy Kingdom come thy will be done on earth just like it is in heaven!" I want to end this chapter with John 14:12 again as a reminder of what Jesus did.

"I tell you the truth, anyone who believes in me will do the same works I have done, and even greater works, because I am going to be with the Father." (John 14:12 NLT)

CHAPTER 4

Different Ways of Healing

Other than Jesus paying for healing on the cross, another reason we know healing is the will of God is because He made so many ways in scripture to receive healing! God didn't just make one way to get healed, but many. Why would God make so many different ways to be healed if it was not His will? After looking at the different types of healings, we see that people are healed in basically 2 different ways. Healing comes either through a miracle or by doing what the Word says and believing it.

First, let me clarify what I mean by miracle. I am talking about the instantaneous healings; limbs grow back, tumors fall off, blind eyes see and deaf ears hear, etc. We all wish we could be healed by a miracle. Although every healing is actually a miracle from God, not every healing occurs instantly. We don't love the part of the verse that says, "lay hands on the sick and they will recover." We want it instantly instead of "will recover" in time.

We don't want to use our faith to see a miracle but instead we would rather rely on the preacher's faith. We would rather drive to a meeting and find someone with the gift of healing and let them lay hands on us instead of standing on what the Word says until healing manifests.

The gift of healing is a great gift and one much needed in the body. It was given to some because at times there is an urgency for healing and some of us don't have enough time to build our faith. Due to living in a fallen world, we have to do the Romans 12:2 thing and renew our mind on healing! It's very easy to forget to stand on the Word for healing when we don't feel good or the doctor has given us a month to live.

The Gift of Healing and Tongues

There are diversities of gifts, but the same Spirit. There are differences of ministries, but the same Lord. And there are diversities of activities, but it is the same God who works all in all. But the manifestation of the Spirit is given to each one for the profit of all: for to one is given the word of wisdom through the Spirit, to another the word of knowledge through the same Spirit, to another faith by the same Spirit, to another gifts of healings by the same Spirit, to another the working of miracles, to another prophecy, to another discerning of spirits, to another different kinds of tongues, to another the interpretation of tongues. But one and the same Spirit works all these things, distributing to each one individually as He wills. (1 Corinthians 12:4-11 NKJV)

This passage shows that there are many gifts given by the Holy Spirit and the gift of healing is just one of them. There are many good books on each gift if you want to research different gifts more. The gift of healing was given for the Body of Christ to strengthen the Church and build our faith. Do we all have the gift of healing? This is tricky because at the end of 1 Corinthians 12 it asks the question, "do all have the gift of healing?"

Now you are the body of Christ, and members
individually. And God has appointed these in the church: first
apostles, second prophets, third teachers, after that miracles, then
gifts of healings, helps, administrations, varieties of tongues. Are
all apostles? Are all prophets? Are all teachers? Are all workers
of miracles? Do all have gifts of healings? Do all speak with
tongues? Do all interpret? But earnestly desire the best gifts. And
yet I show you a more excellent way. (1 Corinthians 12:27-31
NKJV)

Remember that it is the same Spirit that works all of the
gifts and you have that Spirit in you; the Holy Spirit of God. If you
study this in more depth, there is a gift of tongues that is equal to
prophecy; when a word is given in tongues and an interpreter
follows. You need the interpretation because no one would
understand what is being said without it. If every gift is for
building up the body, how would this gift work if no one knew
what was happening? So, the gift of tongues needs the gift of
interpretation.

There is also praying in the Spirit as Paul explains. It
talks about building yourself up in your most holy faith. This does
not need an interpreter because you are not talking to man but to
God and He knows what you are saying. Paul said he wished that
everyone would pray in the Spirit as much as he did but in church
he would rather speak a few words of understanding then talk
with no one understanding.

Tongues can be another way for healing and letting the
Spirit pray a perfect prayer out of your mouth. This also removes
any doubt and fear from your words because if you can't

understand what you are saying then you can't say faithless words. Also, if you remember the importance of dominion from the first chapter, tongues start to make more sense. Why would God need you to pray when you don't even know what you are saying? If it's the Holy Spirit praying to God and they are one, why doesn't God just do it? This is a similar question to, why did God need to come down in the form of a man (Jesus) instead of just waving His hand and fixing it? The answer to both is, God gave man dominion. There is power in what you say on this earth. God is using your voice to pray because He gave us dominion on the earth!

Death and life are in the power of the tongue, And those who love it and indulge it will eat its fruit and bear the consequences of their words. (Proverbs 18:21 AMP)

So, just like the gift of tongues is different from praying in the Spirit, the gift of healing is different from the Biblical promise that we all can receive healing and pray for others' healing. The gift of healing and every gift is from the same Spirit that lives inside all of us so don't ever say "I don't have that gift" when the Holy Spirit can give you whatever gift, at any time, as He needs.

People ask what the best Spiritual gift is and the answer is, the one that is needed at the moment. Everyone will have a gift they operate in more than others but if you usually operate in the word of knowledge and someone needs a healing then let God be God. He can put the gift that is needed on you the moment it's needed. We all have different giftings in the body and it's designed so we work with each other. But the Holy Spirit's gifts are for destroying the works of the devil so God will use anyone who is willing to work with whatever gift is needed at the moment.

For as we have many members in one body, and all members have not the same office: so we, being many, are one body in Christ, and every one members one of another. Having then gifts differing according to the grace that is given to us, whether prophecy, let us prophesy according to the proportion of faith; or ministry, let us wait on our ministering: or he that teacheth, on teaching; or he that exhorteth, on exhortation: he that giveth, let him do it with simplicity; he that ruleth, with diligence; he that sheweth mercy, with cheerfulness. (Romans 12:4-8 KJV)

Now concerning spiritual gifts, brethren, I do not want you to be ignorant: You know that you were Gentiles, carried away to these dumb idols, however you were led. Therefore I make known to you that no one speaking by the Spirit of God calls Jesus accursed, and no one can say that Jesus is Lord except by the Holy Spirit. There are diversities of gifts, but the same Spirit. There are differences of ministries, but the same Lord. And there are diversities of activities, but it is the same God who works all in all. But the manifestation of the Spirit is given to each one for the profit of all: for to one is given the word of wisdom through the Spirit, to another the word of knowledge through the same Spirit, to another faith by the same Spirit, to another gifts of healings by the same Spirit, to another the working of miracles, to another prophecy, to another discerning of spirits, to another different kinds of tongues, to another the interpretation of tongues. But one and the same Spirit works all these things, distributing to each one individually as He wills. For as the body is one and has many members, but all the members of that one body, being many, are one body, so also is Christ. For by one Spirit we were all baptized into one body—whether Jews or Greeks, whether slaves or free— and have all been made to drink into one Spirit. For in fact the body is not one member but many. If the foot should say, "Because I am not a hand, I am not of the body," is it therefore not of the body? And if the ear should say, "Because I am not an eye, I am not of the body," is it therefore not of the body? If the whole body were an eye, where would be the hearing? If the whole were hearing, where would be the smelling? But now God has set the members, each one of them, in the body just as He pleased. And if they were all one member, where would the body be? But now indeed there are many members, yet one body. And the eye cannot say to the hand, "I have no need of you"; nor again the head to the feet, "I have no need of you." No, much rather, those members of the body which seem to be weaker are necessary. And those members of the body which we think to be less honorable, on these we bestow greater honor; and our unpresentable parts have greater modesty, but our presentable parts have no need. But God composed the body, having given greater honor to that part which lacks it, that there should be no schism in the body, but that the members should have the same care for one another. And if one member suffers, all the members suffer with it; or if one member is honored, all the members rejoice with it. Now you are the body of Christ, and members individually. And God has appointed these in the church: first apostles, second prophets, third teachers, after that miracles, then gifts of healings, helps, administrations, varieties of tongues. Are all apostles? Are all prophets? Are all teachers? Are all workers of miracles? Do all have gifts of healings? Do all speak with tongues? Do all interpret? But earnestly desire the best gifts. And yet I show you a more excellent way. (1 Corinthians 12:1-31 NKJV)

Healing Through Faith

Another way to receive healing in addition to the gift of healing and praying in the Spirit is faith. There are a few different ways to be healed by faith. Remember Jesus said many times, without praying for someone, "Your faith has made you well". When I was wondering about healing, I saw miracles in the Bible and I wanted to see if there was a pattern at all. I couldn't see it at first.

There was a woman that touched Jesus and was healed without Him even knowing who touched Him, a man lowered through a roof, a man that said don't come to my house just say the word, handkerchiefs sent, people laid out in the street for the disciples shadow to touch and so many more stories. It's hard to see a pattern until you notice what Jesus said many times, "Your faith has healed you". The miracle happened when someone was believing it would happen.

The pattern was their faith worked and they got their miracle according to their belief and it even happened the way they believed it would. Your faith in the Word will get you your breakthrough. When you get past trying to get God to do something He already did, to believing in what He did, you will begin to change. The devil will try and use the moment between this revelation and your breakthrough to bring doubt. He will say things like, "See it didn't work." Don't listen to him. Don't just have faith in my words, have faith in God's Word! Faith in what was paid for over 2,000 years ago will cause it to manifest now just as believing in Jesus will bring salvation that was paid for on the cross.

But Jesus turned around, and when He saw her He said, "Be of good cheer, daughter; <u>your faith</u> has made you well." And the woman was made well from that hour. (Matthew 9:22 NKJV)

And when He had come into the house, the blind men came to Him. And Jesus said to them, "Do you believe that I am able to do this?" They said to Him, "Yes, Lord." Then He touched their eyes, saying, "According to <u>your faith</u> let it be to you." And their eyes were opened. And Jesus sternly warned them, saying, "See that no one knows it." But when they had departed, they spread the news about Him in all that country. (Matthew 9:28-31 NKJV)

So Jesus answered and said, "Were there not ten cleansed? But where are the nine? Were there not any found who returned to give glory to God except this foreigner?" And He said to him, "Arise, go your way. <u>Your faith</u> has made you well." (Luke 17:17-19 NKJV)

Then He said to her, "Your sins are forgiven." And those who sat at the table with Him began to say to themselves, "Who is this who even forgives sins?" Then He said to the woman, "<u>Your faith</u> has saved you. Go in peace." (Luke 7:48-50 NKJV)

Then it happened, as He was coming near Jericho, that a certain blind man sat by the road begging. And hearing a multitude passing by, he asked what it meant. So they told him that Jesus of Nazareth was passing by. And he cried out, saying, "Jesus, Son of David, have mercy on me!" Then those who went before warned him that he should be quiet; but he cried out all the more, "Son of David, have mercy on me!" So Jesus stood still and commanded him to be brought to Him. And when he had come near, He asked him, saying, "What do you want Me to do for you?" He said, "Lord, that I may receive my sight." Then Jesus said to him, "Receive your sight; your faith has made you well." And immediately he received his sight, and followed Him, glorifying God. And all the people, when they saw it, gave praise to God. (Luke 18:35-43 NKJV)

You see in these stories and many more that Jesus says YOUR faith has healed you. We want God to do everything and we will just sit back and relax. God has done everything He needed to do for you to receive your healing and now we need to learn how to receive what was already done! We have salvation through faith, healing through faith, and blessing through faith. Everything in a Christian's life is of faith. Faith of a mustard seed can move mountains.

Faith is powerful and sometimes it is from other people's faith that we receive healing. The gift of healing is one way other beleiver's faith can bring healing but it can also come through a prayer of faith.

Is anyone among you sick? Let him call for the elders of the church, and let them pray over him, anointing him with oil in the name of the Lord. And the prayer of faith will save the sick, and the Lord will raise him up. And if he has committed sins, he will be forgiven. (James 5:14-15 NKJV)

For where two or three are gathered together in My name, I am there in the midst of them. (Matthew 18:20 NKJV)

And He said to them, "Go into all the world and preach the gospel to every creature. He who believes and is baptized will be saved; but he who does not believe will be condemned. And these signs will follow those who believe: In My name they will cast out demons; they will speak with new tongues; they will take up serpents; and if they drink anything deadly, it will by no means hurt them; they will lay hands on the sick, and they will recover." (Mark 16:15-18 NKJV)

There is power in prayer and power when we come together as Christians. We are commanded to go out into the world and when we do, miracles are promised to follow those who believe. Too often we want to see signs to believe but signs follow the believer. Again, it would be silly to say God save me and I will believe in you. Everyone knows with salvation you must believe first, then salvation comes, yet we want to be healed first in order to believe in healing. This is backwards from what scripture says.

Mark 16 (The Great Commission) isn't a suggestion but a command. We often think the qualifications to see miracles is that we have to be a prophet or maybe an apostle. It says very clearly that the qualifications for miracles to follow you is simply to believe!

You see in James that it talks about coming to the elders if you are sick. Why? There is power when two or three are gathered and pray in faith. There is power in the blood of Jesus and anything that is even a shadow of Jesus has power! Oil in scripture is a representation of the power of God and/or the Holy Spirit. When you are sick, you need to remember that the Word and even just a symbol of God, has power in it! We have the Spirit without measure but it is important, living in a physical body, to have physical symbols for the supernatural.

When the woman with the issue of blood touched Jesus, she touched the hem of His garment that was called the tallit. The tallit was a symbol back then of communal solidarity to their God. In other words, the Pharisees had it as a symbol of their righteousness. When she touched Jesus, she touched His tallit and it was a symbol of His righteousness. The symbol attached to faith was enough for her miracle. The sacrifice of animals was just a symbol of the blood of Jesus but was enough for their sins for the year.

Communion

Another powerful symbol and way to be healed is communion. Communion is a symbol of what Jesus did for us on the cross. It is a symbol of His blood and His body. You might be thinking, "What does that have to do with healing?" To answer that, let's take a look at sacrifices back in the Old Testament for a moment.

When one brought their sacrifices to the priest it had to be perfect, without any blemish. Why? This was a symbol of Jesus's sacrifice, so it had to be perfect. When the priest killed the animal it had to be calm and the family came and put their hands on the animal. This was again a symbol of their sins transferring onto the sacrifice. This also calmed the animal down. The animal needed to be calm because if an animal struggles or fights when it is killed it releases toxins into the blood. Again, this was a symbol of Jesus and His blood for us, so there could be no toxins in the animal's body. The priest would use a very sharp knife so the animal didn't even know it was cut and with the family there, it just died in peace. This would leave the meat perfect for the high priest. Think about this: the sacrifice back then needed to die in a very humane way but Jesus was the opposite. He died a most horrific death. His body was beaten and torn apart. What was the difference with Jesus compared to a lamb?

Surely He has borne our griefs And carried our sorrows; Yet we esteemed Him stricken, Smitten by God, and afflicted. But He was wounded for our transgressions, He was bruised for our iniquities; The chastisement for our peace was upon Him, And by His stripes we are healed. (Isaiah 53:4-5 NKJV)

The shedding of blood was for our sins but the beating of His body was for your body. By His stripes you were healed. He didn't just want to get you into heaven one day but he wanted to reverse the curse of the devil. He wanted to make a way for "Thy kingdom come Thy will be done on earth as it is in heaven". He went all the way for you and it was a high price for healing in all that He went through.

You might think a bit differently about how you pray now knowing He went through being ripped apart for you to be healed (wounded for transgressions, bruised for iniquities and stripes for healing). He went through all of that and we get angry that He isn't healing us or healing doesn't work. We need to realize that the problem is not on the supernatural side but it's on the natural side of our receiving. Trying to receive the perfect (supernatural) in this fallen world can be difficult. So, communion is a symbol of His blood and His body. We take communion to remember what He did and renew our mind about our salvation and healing.

For I received from the Lord that which I also delivered to you: that the Lord Jesus on the same night in which He was betrayed took bread; and when He had given thanks, He broke it and said, "Take, eat; this is My body which is broken for you; do this in remembrance of Me." In the same manner He also took the cup after supper, saying, "This cup is the new covenant in My blood. This do, as often as you drink it, in remembrance of Me." For as often as you eat this bread and drink this cup, you proclaim the Lord's death till He comes. (1 Corinthians 11:23-26 NKJV)

Therefore whoever eats this bread or drinks this cup of the Lord in an unworthy manner will be guilty of the body and blood of the Lord. But let a man examine himself, and so let him eat of the bread and drink of the cup. For he who eats and drinks in an unworthy manner eats and drinks judgment to himself, not discerning the Lord's body. For this reason many are weak and sick among you, and many sleep. (1 Corinthians 11:27-30 NKJV)

These verses in First Corinthians 11 can be a scary if you don't understand what it's talking about. At first glance you can read it and think, "If I am unworthy and I take communion I will die." This is where that Indiana Jones scene comes from; if he wasn't worthy and drank from the cup then he would die. This couldn't be farther from the truth. The blood and body of Jesus was for sinners that wanted to accept it and we were all unworthy of the free gift He gave for us.

What this verse is saying is that many are weak and sick among you and many sleep (which means they died) because of the line right before. The line that says, "he who eats and drinks in an unworthy manner eats and drinks judgment to himself." We need to find out what an unworthy manner means then. It is spelled out for us in the phrase, "not discerning the body." People are this way not because they took communion with sin in their lives but because they didn't discern the body of Jesus correctly.

We need to realize if we don't know that, "by His stripes you were healed" we'll settle for sickness. Discerning the body is looking at both parts and remembering the value in both parts. Imagine you buy a new truck with a pull behind trailer and only sit in the truck. It's great to have a new truck but there is so much you are missing when you forget the trailer. Salvation is the greatest gift in the world and if you forget that healing is included, you will be missing out. Included is not just salvations and healing but also that Shalom we talked about!

Salvation in the Greek is the word Sozo and is much more than we think. The King James Version of the new testament was originally translated from a Greek manuscript. A word study done on a specific Greek word can better determine its exact meaning. So, when the Greek word is understood in depth, the meaning of different verses becomes more clear. As an example, consider the Greek word Sozo which has been translated in the New Testament the following ways:

1. save or saved

2. whole

3. healed

4. preserve

5. well

So, when we take communion it is a symbol of what Jesus did and what salvation fully means. We remember the blood and the body and what they are both for; forgiveness of sins and healing! Remember that even a symbol of the power of God was enough before Jesus died. How much more now when we have the Holy Spirit!

When the woman touched the hem of Jesus's garment (the symbol of His righteousness) with faith, she was healed. Remember Jesus had not died yet at this time. The sacrifices offered were symbols before Jesus died. The Isrealites ate the

Passover supper before they left Egypt. They put a symbol of the blood of Jesus over the door post and the angel of death passed by. It says in Psalms 105:37 that there were none weak among them! How can you be slaves your whole life without good food, working in the hot sun, getting whipped, and then all of a sudden you walk out strong? It was the symbol of Jesus. Just that shadow of Jesus was enough to heal their bodies from malnutrition, getting beat and more! This is why we discern the body! So communion is a symbol for today so we never forget.

He brought them forth also with silver and gold: And there was not one feeble person among their tribes. (Psalm 105:37 KJV)

My people are destroyed for lack of knowledge. Because you have rejected knowledge, I also will reject you from being priest for Me; Because you have forgotten the law of your God, I also will forget your children. (Hosea 4:6 NKJV)

My people are destroyed for lack of knowledge. That sounds a lot like, many are weak and even die not discerning the body! People say "what you don't know, won't hurt" when in fact the Bible says what you don't know will kill you! Another saying is, "what doesn't kill you, makes you stronger". When we remain in sickness we often experience more doubt instead of strength. It is important to discern the Lord's body and know and remember ALL that he did for us on the cross. God is not destroying us for our lack of knowledge but our lack of knowledge will allow Satan a foothold to destroy us when we don't recognize and receive all Jesus has done.

Even so it is not the will of your Father who is in heaven that one of these little ones should perish. (Matthew 18:14 NKJV)

We see that it is God's will that not one person end up in hell but we know that some people still choose that. So, we can also believe that it is God's will that not one person be sick and yet sickness attacks every day. God actually wants us healed more than we want to be healed. We just need to act to bring it from the supernatural to the natural, bringing His Kingdom to earth as it is in heaven. We need to receive what was already paid for the way the Bible says to. If we try to get God to do what He already did or commanded us to do, it will leave us very frustrated. But the good news is God wants us healed so much, He made several ways for us to access it. We just have to learn and act on what He promised us.

Beloved, I pray that you may prosper in all things and be in health, just as your soul prospers. (3 John 1:2 NKJV)

Obedience

I know telling people to obey is not usually met with an enthusiastic response, but it is actually a very effective way of receiving healing for many cases. In fact it is one of the very first promises the Lord made with His people when He created the law with them.

So you shall serve the Lord your God, and He will bless your bread and your water. And I will take sickness away from the midst of you. (Exodus 23:25 NKJV)

In this chapter, the Lord is telling the Hebrew people what His standards are for serving Him. But He also tells them the benefits and promises He has for those who walk according to His commandments. We are promised healing when we walk according to the Lord's standards.

Many people think that obedience is only about the spiritual aspect of following God's commands but God actually has lots of advice for every part of your life including the physical.

When you look at the laws He laid out for the Hebrew people in Exodus, Leviticus, and Deuteronomy, a lot of them cover very practical ways of taking care of our bodies. The hygiene and disease control concepts of the Law was way ahead of its time. So, even if we are no longer under the law, there is still an element of wisdom that we can follow in how we treat our bodies now with the ample information we have about what is and isn't good for us.

I know of a man who exercised this concept to receive his own healing. After being diagnosed with non-Hodgkins lymphoma cancer, he was told by doctors that it was incurable and even with successful treatment he had only a few years left to live. But he refused to accept this as the final diagnosis and dove into the Word of God to lay hold of his healing.

While he was seeking the Lord and standing on several healing scriptures daily, he felt the Holy Spirit prompt him to make some lifestyle changes. He found some teaching from a Christian nutritionist that revealed how a number of the kosher eating practices are actually aligned with recently discovered nutritional facts the Jewish people would have had no way of knowing at the time. Through this teaching the Lord led him to permanently cut out certain toxic ingredients and adopt other kosher habits such as not eating any pork or bottom feeding shellfish. Now, this may all seem random but there have been studies that show how toxic the meat in pork, shrimp, lobster, and crabs actually is for you because they are creatures that consume waste as their primary source of food (Qamar M. F., 2012).

This man was determined to make dietary changes and commit to follow them even after he received his healing. Now, 20 years later, he is in complete remission and continues to follow these guidelines the Lord gave him.

Sometimes I wonder if people experience their miraculous healing only to lose it because they ignore the leading of the Spirit to be better stewards of His temple? Or even if some have not yet received their healing because they will not do what the Lord has set before them, simple lifestyle changes that can make all the difference. Staying active, sleeping enough, and eating right are all part of a system the Lord has put in place to keep your body functioning at prime performance. If we ignore these, it can make it hard to receive the healing the Lord has for us.

This is also laid out in scripture in several different ways, one being what I already mentioned in the law that was given to the Jewish people. Now remember we are not under the old law any longer, we are under the grace in Christ Jesus. But Jesus did mention that the truth laid out in the Old Covenant remains true. We are redeemed from the curse of the law but the promises and blessings can still be ours! Why is this? Jesus didn't get rid of the law but fulfilled it! The qualifications of the blessings back in Deuteronomy was to keep all of the commandments. If you are in Christ you also have the fulfillment of the law in you through the blood of Jesus; that blood covenant, tribal alliance we talked about.

For assuredly, I say to you, till heaven and earth pass away, one jot or one tittle will by no means pass from the law till all is fulfilled. (Matthew 5:18)

What that means for us today is that we will no longer be condemned for sinning because we haven't followed the law to the letter since it was fulfilled in Christ already. However, God has still given us His word to follow so that we can have an abundant life and walk in His perfect peace. If you want to receive the promises in the scripture, you have to apply it to your life.

That looks different and happens at different degrees for everyone. One man may struggle with smoking and has not yet received the conviction from the Lord to quit, while another man may struggle with laziness and has not yet grown to exercise regularly. What this really boils down to is, you have to listen to what the Spirit is leading you to do. Perhaps that looks like cutting something like sugar out of your diet, or adding something like more vegetables into it. Or maybe that looks like cutting the time you spend watching TV before bed in order to fall asleep sooner and get more rest.

I think Daniel is another great example of following the Lord's convictions which led him and his friends to have better health than those around them.

But Daniel purposed in his heart that he would not defile himself with the portion of the king's delicacies, nor with the wine which he drank; therefore he requested of the chief of the eunuchs that he might not defile himself...
...At the end of ten days their features appeared better and fatter in flesh than all the young men who ate the portion of the king's delicacies. Thus the steward took away their portion of delicacies and the wine that they were to drink, and gave them vegetables. (Daniel 1:9,15-16)

Sometimes, obedience doesn't always make sense either. I think of the story where Jesus healed the man born blind.

When He had said these things, He spat on the ground and made clay with the saliva; and He anointed the eyes of the blind man with the clay. And He said to him, "Go, wash in the pool of Siloam." So he went and washed, and came back seeing. (John 9:6-7)

I wonder what would have happened if that man had just decided not to follow Jesus' instructions? Or if he just did things his own way and washed in a different place? Would he have received his healing? Perhaps, but I think that when the Lord gives a command, it is always with intention and for a very specific purpose. We do not serve an arbitrary God and His Word does not go forth from

Him in vain. So, when he gives you something to do, it is usually for a good reason.

If you have not seen your healing, and you have been in every prayer line for years, and you have been standing in faith, would you perhaps consider that maybe the Lord has had something He has been trying to tell you to do? He wants to give you healing more than anything, but sometimes we are standing in our own way. Consider asking the Holy Spirit if there are some lifestyle changes he'd like you to make. And even if you do not need healing right now, ask the Lord what things He may have for you to change so that you won't weaken your body unto sickness. He wants to help you in every area of your life, sometimes it just takes obedience.

CHAPTER 5

Why Does Healing Seem to Only Work Sometimes?

I know if you have been a Chistian for any extended period of time, you have probably seen people get prayed for and then nothing happened or even worse, maybe even die. I have prayed for people and seen miracles happen and I have also prayed for people that never got better. This can be very frustrating and may even make you not want to pray for anyone again.

We need to remember Mark 16. The Great Commission is not a suggestion but a command. We are to go into all the world and preach the gospel. One of the signs that is promised to you, if you believe, is that you will lay hands on the sick and they will recover. We need to get our emotions out of the way with what God has asked us to do. God is moved by faith and obedience and not by feelings. We want to worship when we feel like it. We want to pray when we feel like it and we only want to pray for others when we feel like it.

I heard a man of God say one day that he was asked the question, "What if you were praying for someone and they dropped dead?" His response was, "I would step over them and pray for the next person." He then said, "If I pray for someone and they get healed do I get credit? So why would I take credit if they didn't get healed." Then he said, "All we need to do is be obedient to what God told us to do. We think that when healing is happening we should feel something different and sometimes you do, but not every time. It is more than a feeling. It's God working through you by your faith and obedience."

Doing Our Part

I want to look at some of the reasons why sometimes we don't see healings happen. One obvious reason is lack of faith; but let's look at a few things. Remember back when we discussed dominion? God gave dominion over to man, but then through sin man gave dominion to Satan. We also covered the wrong teaching on sovereignty and we understand that although God is sovereign (all powerful) He is not all controlling. He works within the boundaries of His Word. If He said it, He will do it. So when Adam and Eve sinned this really messed things up. The devil got their dominion. We are going to break down the book of Job a bit in a different chapter but look at Job 1:6-7 real quick.

Now there was a day when the sons of God came to present themselves before the LORD, and Satan came also among them. And the LORD said unto Satan, Whence comest thou? Then Satan answered the LORD, and said, From going to and fro in the earth, and from walking up and down in it. (Job 1:6-7 KJV)

At first glance this might not seem like anything but why was Satan in heaven when God had already thrown him out? In Revelation chapter 12, it says that Satan fell like lightning to earth. Then in Genesis, we see him in the garden talking with Eve. How in the world could Satan then be back in heaven talking with God in the book of Job? He took Adam's dominion so he had Adam's right to be there. Satan is running the show down here. This might mess up your theology but it is in the Bible. Let's look at some verses that show the devil still has dominion on earth.

But if our gospel be hid, it is hid to them that are lost: in whom the god of this world hath blinded the minds of them which believe not, lest the light of the glorious gospel of Christ, who is the image of God, should shine unto them. (2 Corinthians 4:3-4 KJV)

I will no longer talk much with you, for the ruler of this world is coming, and he has nothing in Me. (John 14:30 NKJV)

Jesus answered and said, "This voice did not come because of Me, but for your sake. Now is the judgment of this world; now the ruler of this world will be cast out. And I, if I am lifted up from the earth, will draw all peoples to Myself." (John 12:30-32 NKJV)

You are of God, little children, and have overcome them, because He who is in you is greater than he who is in the world. (1 John 4:4 NKJV)

There are many more verses like this but I hope you get the point. We see that the devil is in the world and has dominion but with Jesus' resurrection, greater is He that is in me then he that is in the world! This is why when people ask, "why do bad things happen to good people?" You can say, "Why don't bad things happen even more often to good people?"

We read John 10:10 and know the devil only comes to steal, kill, and destroy. So, if he is in the world and that is his only mission, you can see why sometimes healing doesn't happen. We have more power and authority than the devil through Jesus, but we sometimes forget that!

Three-Part Beings

Another reason healing sometimes seems sporadic is because we live in a fallen world. With the devil out to steal, kill, and destroy, we need to stand and fight for healing. God usually works through us. Don't get me wrong; it's 100% His power, but it comes through us. The Holy Spirit lives on the inside and flows through us as we let Him. We are imperfect vessels with the power of God working through our obedience. He is perfect but we are still in the flesh and are not perfect.

We are made in the image of God and He is a three-part being and so are we. We are a spirit, we have a soul, and we live in a body. You have to understand that you are a spirit. That is who you really are. Your spirit can live without your body but your body can not live without your spirit. If your spirit leaves, your body would fall to the ground. Your spirit is the saved part of you with the blood of Jesus on it. We are righteous because He is righteous. This is why Romans 12:2 places such an emphasis on renewing your mind.

Your spirit is the God-part that is going to heaven. What this means is that this is the part of you that is able to be connected to the divine. We know that in the beginning before Adam and Eve sinned, they had perfect communion with God because their spirits were alive. So, when God told them that they would die if they ate the fruit of the tree of the knowledge of good and evil, He was talking about their spirits. Paul explains this in Romans 5. What that means is that because of their sin, all of us are dead in our spirit. Before we were saved, we had no way to be in communion with God because our spirit was dead. But when we accept salvation, the God-part of us is reborn so we can now have connection to the divine again. This God-part is our saved part that is righteous due to our acceptance of Jesus.

We Are a 3-Part Whole

We are spirit, have a soul and live in a body

-chart from Faith and Health connection

Your body does not get saved but gets older everyday. This does not mean you need to accept sickness just that you will get older. The Word says that Moses was still strong at death.

Your soul is your mind, will, and emotions. This is what people often struggle to control. Our mind, will, and emotions are all over the place when we don't stay in the Word. Our emotions change–not just daily–but sometimes even by the minute. If we don't keep them in check, they will control our life. Our spirit, the God-part, should be running our life but we have it backwards.

We want to believe in healing for our body but our body tells us what to do. Jesus spoke to bodies and told them to be healed. He spoke to blind eyes and told them to open. We want to do the same but too often our body dictates perception. It tells you when you're hungry, tired, or even feeling sick. It will get you up in the middle of the night for a snack or make you stop what you are doing to go take a nap. Your body was designed this way for a reason so it's not always a bad thing; we just need to keep it in check.

We are a three-part being and we are responsible for all three parts. Some people get saved but don't renew their mind and so their life doesn't change like it should and then they don't get the results they want and are angry at God. Then some people get saved but don't take care of themselves in practical ways physically, so they don't last as long as they should. I would say the majority of things people ask me to pray for healing over could be "healed" by simply taking care of their body. God created your body with the ability to heal on its own from many issues… if it is given the proper nutrients and care.

But He also gave us free will. This is where a lot of people lose their healing. We as a country put so much junk into our bodies. Think of how much cancer, diabetes, heart disease, and so many other health complications are running rampant because of the unhealthy habits that are just accepted as normal.This is not meant to condemn anyone but to make us realize it's not God's fault. We also have a responsibility to take care of the body He has given us. God can and will still heal us because healing works but sometimes He does that through our obedience. When we do the natural and He does the supernatural there is power.

Most people wouldn't go play in the road with a blindfold and ask God to protect them. But think about how many people are perfectly fine eating fast food, drinking energy drinks and soda all the time but then wonder why God isn't healing them. I have had people ask me to pray over their breathing but they won't stop smoking. I've had people ask me to pray over their back pain but they are a hundred pounds overweight.

God loves to heal but if we don't obey the natural laws He put in place, we are using our free will to get out of God's best for our lives. We take care of our Spirit by changing our path and following Christ which is salvation. We take care of our soul by renewing our minds in the Word, meditating on it, speaking it and surrounding ourselves with like minded people. But we also need to take care of our body by watching what we put in it and staying active. It's amazing how much natural healing could happen in your body by just making these simple lifestyle changes. This is not belittling the power of God to heal supernaturally but it does show us how much He wants us well. So much so, that He even programmed natural ways for healing to happen into our body's make-up. If He made our bodies with the ability to heal themselves, how much does that speak to the fact that healing is His will!

We are saved by believing what Jesus did for us and by putting our hope in Him. It's not that our spirit is healed but that it is completely regenerated; brand new. Now, we need healing in our other two parts; healing in our soul, (mind, will, and emotions), and healing in our physical bodies. So, when people read scripture and say certain verses are talking about spiritual healing, that is not the case. When God regenerates your spirit, it is a done deal. However, we do need healing in our thoughts, emotions, desires, and from sickness in our bodies.

But you are not in the flesh but in the Spirit, if indeed the Spirit of God dwells in you. Now if anyone does not have the Spirit of Christ, he is not His. And if Christ is in you, the body is dead because of sin, but the Spirit is life because of righteousness. But if the Spirit of Him who raised Jesus from the dead dwells in you, He who raised Christ from the dead will also give life to your mortal bodies through His Spirit who dwells in you. (Romans 8:9-11 NKJV)

Look at how Romans 8 lays it all out; you are now not in the flesh if Christ is in you! You are a spirit and we are trying to get our bodies healed. The Spirit that dwells in us is righteous and brings life to our mortal bodies. This does not mean one day in heaven, because that would be a glorified body that doesn't need healing. Righteousness is why you can receive healing! It is not your righteousness because that is self-righteousness. It is His righteousness living in us that will touch and bring life to our mortal (earthly) bodies! This should get us excited. So how does this work?

For those who live according to the flesh set their minds on the things of the flesh, but those who live according to the Spirit, the things of the Spirit. For to be carnally minded is death, but to be spiritually minded is life and peace. (Romans 8:5-6 NKJV)

When you are in Christ, Romans 8:1 says that there is no condemnation for you if you walk according to the Spirit and not the flesh. Then Romans 8:9 says, we are in the Spirit if the Spirit of God dwells in us. So, at salvation you are not in the flesh anymore but in the Spirit, which means there is no condemnation for you. You are righteous because He is righteous.

Now, look back at Romans 8:6 which states to be carnally minded (thinking about things of the world) is death but to be spiritually minded (thinking about things of God, your free gift of righteousness) is life and peace. This peace is also translated from that Hebrew word we talked about before, Shalom; peace, healing, wholeness, completeness, and prosperity. To say it simply; we are a three-part being. We are a spirit and live in a body. Our soul (mind, will and emotions) is in between the two. When we fix our mind on things of the Spirit, there is life (healing) for our mortal bodies!

Fasting

We are a three-part being and this is the reason we are told to fast. We have been taught fasting wrong for a long time. I used to think you fasted to get God to do something. But remember, God already did it all 2,000 years ago. We fast like

Pharisees trying to get God's attention so He will answer us. He already said ask anything in my name and it will be done! The Pharisees used to go outside the gates, tear their clothes and throw dirt on themselves to get God's attention. We have God's attention, we just need to follow His Word.

We think fasting will get us closer to God. We don't fast to get closer to God but to discipline our flesh (soul and body). If fasting was to get closer to God then why did Jesus fast? He was fully God and fully man. Jesus fasted before He started the work on earth He came to do; primarily going to the cross. He went 40 days without food. Most scholars will say that at that point the body is basically dead and starts to eat itself. Jesus killed His flesh because they were about to rip Him apart. Jesus could have come down from the cross at anypoint but He didn't because He had control of His flesh.

We fast to tell our bodies "no" so that when we tell our body to line up with the Word of God it listens. I've seen people fast from other things besides food. It's great to give up something that we like to remind us how much more Christ means to us but if we want healing in our body we need to get it into submission. Fasting food obviously has a direct impact on the body.

Being a three-part being we see that our spirit is the God-part. Our soul can be brought into order just as Romans 12:2 says; renew your mind to the Word of God. Our body is the shell we live in that does get older every day. This doesn't mean that we need to be sick but we will age. The body is in the natural and is the part that has senses. So our Spirit is renewed at salvation, our soul we should renew everyday to the Word of God and the Body we work on through eating right and exercising. Fasting is needed when you are trying to discipline your soul or body. If you are having thoughts often that you know are not from God, struggling with what you are looking at or an addiction, fasting is a great way to take back control. The fight is for our mind (soul). This is why God says to take every thought captive. The devil is going to attack you in your soul or body to try and get you to believe something against the Word.

Now, I want to briefly remind you though that it is not our own righteousness that gives us access to promises of God, it is faith in God's righteousness. Think about this; Abraham believed God and it was accounted to him as righteousness. What does this mean?

Have you suffered so many things in vain—if indeed it was in vain? Therefore He who supplies the Spirit to you and works miracles among you, does He do it by the works of the law, or by the hearing of faith?—just as Abraham "believed God, and it was accounted to him for righteousness." Therefore know that only those who are of faith are sons of Abraham. (Galatians 3:4-7 NKJV)

Who, contrary to hope, in hope believed, so that he became the father of many nations, according to what was spoken, "So shall your descendants be." And not being weak in faith, he did not consider his own body, already dead (since he was about a hundred years old), and the deadness of Sarah's womb. He did not waver at the promise of God through unbelief, but was strengthened in faith, giving glory to God, and being fully convinced that what He had promised He was also able to perform. And therefore "it was accounted to him for righteousness." (Romans 4:18-22 NKJV)

We think we need to be righteous to receive our healing so we fast or we do things to make us "worthy" but Abraham was considered righteous before the blood of Jesus just for believing (faith) in what God said. Abraham wasn't believing for something as simple as a headache, He was believing that God could give him a child after his body was too old. Scripture says he didn't waver in faith but gave praise to God for Isacc before he was even there.

This is huge because from the time God made the promise to Abraham to the time Isacc showed up was 25 years! Could you praise God for something for 25 years before it came? Could you praise God for healing for a year before it actually manifested? This is faith. And when you have faith in what God said, (like by His stripes we are healed) it will manifest.

Faith is what makes it happen and faith comes by hearing and hearing by the Word of God. So, when you declare something, you are not faking it until you make it, you are calling those things that are not as though they were. You are building faith.

Praise builds faith. Praise isn't about trying to say the right things to get what you want to manifest. Praise is when you see what God said in the supernatural and that becomes more real to you then what you see in the natural world. How do you know when it becomes real to you? When you are able to thank God before it gets there. Our prayer is often proof of our unbelief but praise is proof of our faith! Look at some of the prayers we pray. We ask God to be with us for the day when He said I will never leave you or forsake you. Instead we could pray thanking God for being with us today! Just change our thinking a little. We pray and beg God's help in our health, mind, finances and so much more because we don't believe the promises that He already promised to do. Most of the time people want prayer over their emotions instead of renewing their mind.

If I called you and said I'm sending you a check, it should be there soon, you would get excited if you believed me. The excitement isn't fake even when everyone around you can't see the check. It's real to you before it gets there because I said I would send it.

The problem is we confuse faith with a vending machine. We act like saying the right things or doing the right actions will make what we are hoping for happen. We come to God and want Him to show us a miracle so we can believe in miracles. This is again not condemnation but you need to learn this. This is a process and we should never let the devil tell us we are doing it wrong. We need to just believe God and renew our mind, standing in faith until our heart is changed by the Word to manifest a miracle!

And when they had come to the multitude, a man came to Him, kneeling down to Him and saying, "Lord, have mercy on my son, for he is an epileptic and suffers severely; for he often falls into the fire and often into the water. So I brought him to Your disciples, but they could not cure him." Then Jesus answered and said, "O faithless and perverse generation, how long shall I be with you? How long shall I bear with you? Bring him here to Me." And Jesus rebuked the demon, and it came out of him; and the child was cured from that very hour. Then the disciples came to Jesus privately and said, "Why could we not cast it out?" So Jesus said to them, *"Because of your unbelief; for assuredly, I say to you, if you have faith as a mustard seed, you will say to this mountain, 'Move from here to there,' and it will move; and nothing will be impossible for you. However, this kind does not go out except by prayer and fasting." (Matthew 17:14-21 NKJV)*

At first glance you read this story and think, "So to get some demons out, we fast?" This is not what Jesus said at all. This story is not about a demon but about unbelief. Jesus starts off by saying "O faithless and perverse generation." He was talking about their lack of faith. When the disciples asked Jesus in private, "Why couldn't we cast out the demon?", He immediately said, "Because of your unbelief". Then Jesus begins teaching about faith the size of a mustard seed. So, when Jesus says, "However, this kind only comes out by prayer and fasting", Jesus wasn't saying this was an extra strong demon, He was talking about their unbelief! O faithless generation if you have faith anything is possible but to get unbelief out of your life, fast and pray! We fast to tell the natural "no" so that the supernatural will flow!

Healing is sometimes sporadic because God is using us. This isn't just with healing but all the gifts of the Spirit. In the Old Testament, the Holy Spirit would fall on people and they would operate in one of His gifts. In the New Testament, the Holy Spirit lives within us so now what is perfect is working through our imperfections. In Deuteronomy it said that if a prophet gave a false

Word from the Lord, they were to stone him. But in the New Testament, we all have the Holy Spirit in us and we are working through these earthen vessels.

Love never fails. But whether there are prophecies, they will fail; whether there are tongues, they will cease; whether there is knowledge, it will vanish away. For we know in part and we prophesy in part. But when that which is perfect has come, then that which is in part will be done away. When I was a child, I spoke as a child, I understood as a child, I thought as a child; but when I became a man, I put away childish things. For now we see in a mirror, dimly, but then face to face. Now I know in part, but then I shall know just as I also am known. And now abide faith, hope, love, these three; but the greatest of these is love. (1 Corinthians 13:8-13 NKJV)

First Corinthians 13 says that we see as in a mirror dimly. This means we can't see everything. So, we do not stone a prophet any more if they miss it. All of the gifts from the Spirit are perfect but moving through us they don't always function like they should. We need to train the gifts through turning off the world and getting closer to God. If you are consumed by the world and have fear and doubt in your life, don't be surprised if the healing isn't happening like it should.

If God is moved by faith, we need to be in faith when praying for others. Andrew Wommack tells a story about raising a woman's husband from the dead. He said he got the call to come pray with a man so he went a few minutes across town to his house. When he got there the man was laying down so Andrew said, "In the name of Jesus," and the man sat up. Then, the woman told Andrew that her husband had died.

Andrew said later he was so glad he didn't know the man was dead because on the short ride over to the house it would have been enough time for him to get into fear and doubt. Sometimes, we can be in faith until we see someone coming toward us in a wheelchair. Our natural senses play a big part in how we react to everything and we need to keep them in check. The more time you spend with God, the more your gift and faith will come alive!

Unbelief: Miracle Killer

Unbelief, doubt, and fear are the number one miracle killers today! But how do we move in faith when most people are struggling with knowing if it's even God's will for them to be healed? When you pray for someone, just be obedient. You don't know what people are dealing with in their hearts. I've seen people totally healed and in a day or two sickness came right back because they let fear creep into their hearts. Even Jesus dealt with people and their unbelief.

Now it came to pass, when Jesus had finished these parables, that He departed from there. When He had come to His own country, He taught them in their synagogue, so that they were astonished and said, "Where did this Man get this wisdom and these mighty works? Is this not the carpenter's son? Is not His mother called Mary? And His brothers James, Joses, Simon, and Judas? And His sisters, are they not all with us? Where then did this Man get all these things?" So they were offended at Him. But Jesus said to them, "A prophet is not without honor except in his own country and in his own house." Now He did not do many mighty works there because of their unbelief. (Matthew 13:53-58 NKJV)

You see, even Jesus was limited because of their unbelief. We don't always know what others are going through so when we don't see an instant miracle, the devil loves to put guilt on us. Whether we did something wrong or they did, we need to be obedient and stay in faith. The Word of God is the best healer and if we can get people to stay out of fear and stand on the Word, healing will happen.

You need to stand on God's word no matter what others say. This includes doctors! Yes, doctors know what is going on in the natural and God can use doctors for healing as well but that does not go above the Word of God.

Remember when God told Moses to take the Israelites into the promised land? God had brought them through miracle after miracle and then He told them to take the land He had promised them. Instead of listening, Moses sent in spies to get man's opinion on what God said. Out of the 12 men sent in, only two of them believed God; Joshua and Caleb. The other ten said, "we look like grasshoppers in their sight!" In other words, "this situation looks impossible."

Even though Moses had seen God do miracle after miracle, he didn't go in and do what God said and they wandered in the desert for 40 years until all the unbelief died out. The only two men that went in were Joshua and Caleb. Sometimes before you can enter into your place of rest you need to kill off unbelief. This means be careful what you listen to and be careful who you talk to.

One of the biggest mistakes of today is people making social media their place to vent. Whenever people have a sickness, problem, or are struggling with something, people love to post it and "ask for prayer." Why do we do this? Why would we want people to know? Just to see how much attention we can get? Your situation isn't everyone's business. Do you think by clicking "like" they are praying and fighting on your behalf? Most of the time people are just gossiping; declaring what sickness you have to everyone without claiming healing in faith.

When God says something, you do not need everyone's input as well. I'm not saying don't go to doctors at all. I am saying use the info that the doctor has given you to know how to pray. Don't get in fear over what the doctor says but use it as a tool to pray; also listen if he says to do something. You need to go off of your faith and what you believe. I love doctors and in fact most Christians would be dead without them because we don't study the Word and do what it says. We pray once, move on, and say "I tried". You can't go to the gym for a day or a week and say I knew this wouldn't work.

I would rather have a few close friends that know who they are in Christ pray for me than announce on social media where everyone, Christians and and non-Christians alike, will see it. Most people don't even know how to pray the Word or pray effectively. I have a few pastors and friends/family I would have stand with me. People that know what the Word says and if I start to get down or in doubt they stand me back up again. Some people go back to thinking like the Pharisees; if they can cry out loud and long enough, God will hear them. If they get enough people praying, surely God will answer their prayers. Again, this is trying to convince God to do something He's already done.

Some friends of mine that I would have stand with me are Joseph Z and his wife Heather. They have a ministry called Zministries and he is a prophet that speaks to leaders all over the world.

Years ago Heather was diagnosed with kidney failure. She needed a new kidney but didn't qualify for a donor. Things began to get worse and they needed a miracle. She was in and out of the doctor's every few days on dialysis. She was watching other patients die around her. Things didn't look good as time went on. She would go to different prayer meetings and get better but wouldn't be totally healed.

One night she went to an Andrew Wommack meeting and received prayer from Andrew. She said that she knew she was healed. She decided not to go into dialysis anymore. It was a huge risk if she wasn't healed; one missed appointment would leave her severely ill. The doctors said if she missed two she would be dead.

She continued to check her levels and they were getting better. She missed an appointment and then two. Then, she missed a week of appointments and then a few weeks. But her body was getting better and better everyday. They were both standing in faith and her body was healed!

After a few months they started to tell a few people close to them. One person very close to them said, "What are you doing? You will kill yourself if your not careful!" This opened up the door to fear. She was healed and had gone without going to the doctor when she should have been dead and yet she was getting better and better everyday.

Joseph started to ask her throughout the day, "Do you still feel good? Are you sure?" She began to question if she was really healed or if she needed to go in to see a doctor. Eventually she was back at the hospital on dialysis. Fear and doubt crept in and they needed a miracle again. God did bring another miracle and she was able to get a transplant. She is doing very well today and the ministry is stronger than ever.

It's with her permission I tell you her story because not everyone is in the same solace in faith and the devil will use whatever he can to steal, kill, and destroy. His primary objective is to get us to not believe the Word like he has done time and time again. Even Jesus had to look at Peter and say, "Get behind me satan." People around you might not be trying to make you afraid. Sometimes they even think they have your best interest in mind but that still doesn't mean they won't say something stupid in the moment. Be careful who you bring into battle with you because well intentioned people can still get you killed in battle. You want seasoned veterans with you that have done battle before and know how to win.

CHAPTER 6

Faith vs Fear

If any of you lacks wisdom, let him ask of God, who gives to all liberally and without reproach, and it will be given to him. But let him ask in faith, with no doubting, for he who doubts is like a wave of the sea driven and tossed by the wind. For let not that man suppose that he will receive anything from the Lord; he is a double-minded man, unstable in all his ways. (James 1:5-8 NKJV)

Faith and fear cannot coexist. You cannot be standing in faith with doubt and fear in your life. James tells us that a double minded man is unstable in all his ways. We have all been in a spot where we know the things we should pray and believe but our heart doesn't fully believe it yet. In James it explains what being double minded is; praying and asking God with doubt in your heart.

It's possible to be double minded about any part of scripture which will be frustrating because you won't see breakthrough, at least not at the level you could. If you have one foot in the law and one foot in grace the Bible will be very confusing. If you are believing God for healing but you're not sure if it's His will, it will be hard for healing to manifest. You can read verses that say, "God is the one that gave man the power to gain wealth" and "my God shall supply all my needs according to His riches and glory.", but if you still question that He wants you blessed this will very possibly prevent your breakthrough from happening.

If we go back and forth on the promises of God, that is double minded. If you have a 700-pound horse pulling on a rope in one direction and another 700-pound horse pulling in the other direction, it's going to be very hard to make much progress. This is where most people in the church find themselves. They pull with faith and live in fear then get frustrated and think the Bible isn't working.

Most people think that Christians "fake it til they make it." This means when we say we are healed in Jesus name and yet don't feel healed, we are just faking it. It says in Romans 10:17, "So then faith comes by hearing, and hearing by the word of God." Sometimes, we are not just saying words to say words but we are "calling those things that are not as though they were" (Romans 4:17) and we build our faith that way. Saying scripture when you don't see the results yet is not faking; it's called faith.

Now faith is the substance of things hoped for, the evidence of things not seen. (Hebrews 11:1 NKJV)

Hebrews tells us that faith is the substance which means an actual physical matter or material. It also says that faith is the evidence of the unseen. When you want to prove if something is wrong or right you look at the evidence or proof to see what is correct. Hebrews tells us that it's your faith that is the proof of something you haven't seen yet. If faith is the proof and is a physical matter or material, that means that faith is working and building in your life.

Many times, we come forward in faith to receive a healing and it doesn't happen immediately. In Mark 16 we read, "lay hands on the sick and they will recover." Healing may not always happen at that exact moment. When we get prayed for in faith; then faith starts to go to work. Then, we go a day without our miracle and think, "well it didn't work this time." The faith that started to build then stops. We aborted a miracle before it was born and the proof that it was coming was our faith. The miracle never showed up because there wasn't enough evidence.

A good man out of the good treasure of his heart brings forth good; and an evil man out of the evil treasure of his heart brings forth evil. For out of the abundance of the heart his mouth speaks. (Luke 6:45 NKJV)

You can tell if someone is in faith or not by what they are saying when they are not trying to impress anyone. I've heard people "praying in faith" but then crying out loud saying, "God don't take them." It isn't a condemnation thing, just something to watch. If we are going to be in faith, our mouth needs to line up with what we really believe. You can't say, "God will provide" but also say, "I don't know if I'll get through."

But he did not doubt or waver in unbelief concerning the promise of God, but he grew strong and empowered by faith, giving glory to God, being fully convinced that God had the power to do what He had promised. (Romans 4:20-21 AMP)

Abraham was in faith and empowered by faith. He believed in God so much so that he gave thanks to God for Isacc before Isacc was even around! How in the world can we give God praise for something we don't have? His faith was the evidence that Isacc was on the way. This is an example of what God said being greater than what was being seen at the moment. Abraham was over 100 years old and his body shouldn't have been able to reproduce. But he believed God so much that he praised Him.

If you were struggling to pay rent and the richest guy in town heard about it and called to tell you he would cover you, would you be excited? What if he hadn't paid the bill yet? Would you still call your close friends and tell them everything? Most likely you would! This is because you believe that he is going to do what he said. This should be us, but we have a hard time believing in a promise that was written down for us thousands of years ago. All we need to do is believe, yet we struggle and that just shows where our faith is.

When we first started the Kingdom Youth Conference I knew it was going to be expensive but I had met a guy that said he would help us fund it. Well, after the events were on the books and things were moving forward, I then learned he wanted a lot of money back and part of the ministry. I couldn't do that! I was depressed because I knew I was going to lose a lot of money that I didn't have. I had made promises to bands, speakers, venues, built a website, booked hotels and flights and now it looked bad.

I forgot that God had called me to do it and I forgot that He promised to take care of my needs. I laid in bed depressed for weeks. I eventually got sick of my own pity party and started listening to faith filled teaching during the day. After a bit of that, my parents called and said they wanted to help in any way they could and they had a line of credit we could use to start.

At that moment everything felt better. I had hope again that we would be alright. The sad part is, I needed my parents to say I got you when my heavenly Father already said I got you. It showed me where my faith was. We all have times when the natural is more real to us then the supernatural.

For God has not given us a spirit of fear, but of power and of love and of a sound mind. (2 Timothy 1:7 NKJV)

We need to understand that fear isn't from God but it is a spirit that is trying to control us. Faith comes from God and a spirit of fear is from the enemy so we can not live in both. Every time that God brings anything our way, the devil will try and get us to doubt the Word and bring fear.

If faith can create, then fear can also create! You might think this is crazy but look at people around you or maybe your own life. Fear came on you just like faith would, and after you meditated on it for a bit, it happened. Look at the book of Job again and notice that Job was living in fear and it manifested in his life!

For the thing I greatly feared has come upon me, And what I dreaded has happened to me. (Job 3:25 NKJV)

Finally, believers, whatever is true, whatever is honorable and worthy of respect, whatever is right and confirmed by God's word, whatever is pure and wholesome, whatever is lovely and brings peace, whatever is admirable and of good repute; if there is any excellence, if there is anything worthy of praise, think continually on these things [center your mind on them, and implant them in your heart]. (Philippians 4:8 AMP)

What we set our mind on is so important. We can be in faith or fear. The Word is clear to keep our mind on the things of God. When we meditate on the supernatural we will see it happen in our life! Proverbs 23:7 says, "as a man thinks in his heart, so *is* he."

Casting down arguments and every high thing that exalts itself against the knowledge of God, bringing every thought into captivity to the obedience of Christ, (2 Corinthians 10:5 NKJV)

When we take every thought captive it means every thought! We line up everything that goes through our mind; only meditating on things that line up with the Word and throwing out the things that don't.

Remember when the Isrealites were told to go into the promised land and they let fear take hold of them? They meditated on how big the giants were in the land. The spies came back and said, "We look like grasshoppers in their sight.". They could have taken the land easily if they had kept their mind on everything God already did for them along the journey.

That's why it's so important to take every thought captive because we can read the Word but if we don't put our faith in it or we forget what it says, it becomes very difficult to get our miracle. First Corinthians 10 tells us how to win and we can not use carnal weapons to win a spiritual battle! Staying in health is a spiritual battle.

Now I, Paul, myself am pleading with you by the meekness and gentleness of Christ— who in presence am lowly among you, but being absent am bold toward you. But I beg you that when I am present I may not be bold with that confidence by which I intend to be bold against some, who think of us as if we walked according to the flesh. For though we walk in the flesh, we do not war according to the flesh. For the weapons of our warfare are not carnal but mighty in God for pulling down strongholds, casting down arguments and every high thing that exalts itself against the knowledge of God, bringing every thought into captivity to the obedience of Christ, and being ready to punish all disobedience when your obedience is fulfilled. (2 Corinthians 10:1-6 NKJV)

Faith and fear can not be in the same place. Taking every thought captive will keep us in faith and not let that spirit of fear creep in. The devil wants nothing more than for us to stay in fear and keep trying to earn what God has already paid for.

Know Your Adversary

Be sober, be vigilant; because your adversary the devil walks about like a roaring lion, seeking whom he may devour. (1 Peter 5:8 NKJV)

I love preaching on 1 Peter 5:8. When we first look at this scripture, it might not mean too much but when we break down every word, this scripture is loaded. First off, being sober and vigilant means to pay attention and be alert. We know that God's "people perish for lack of knowledge."

Then it goes on to say, "your adversary." This tells us that the devil is not God's adversary but ours! Why? God already defeated the devil. An adversary needs a current battle to exist. There is no fight between God and the devil. God has already finished the devil with no problem at all. So, that means the devil is our enemy; he is after us! Remember his only goal is to steal, kill and destroy you! He does battle with us every day and it happens in our mind.

Next, in 1 Peter it says he walks about "like a roaring lion." So, 'like' a lion means he's not a lion but a fake. He is an imposter. He isn't a real lion but he is seeking whom he can destroy. This tells me he doesn't even know who he can win against! Why? Because the only believers the devil can devour are the ones who don't know who they are in Christ. Every believer has the victory in Christ. So, who we are in Christ doesn't scare the devil. He already knows who we are in Christ. What scares him is that we will figure out who we are in Christ! If we don't know what's on the inside of us, we won't have victory. As soon as we do know, we will have victory.

Why do lions roar? Lions roar to tell other lions their location, to show how big they are, and to warn lions from other prides to stay away from their home territory. They do this mostly just before sunrise and after sunset which is when they are most active. A lion does not actually want to fight, it just wants to scare everything off so it can take the territory (Lindsey, 2021).

Once, I looked up how to survive a lion attack and I could hardly believe what it said! The advice was this:

> *Do not run. Stand your ground. You need to take charge of the situation and show the lion that you're a threat. Turn so that you're side-on-side with the lion while clapping your hands, shouting, and waving your arms. This will make you appear bigger and more threatening to the lion. The lion will know you are the real threat* (Unknown, 2022).

To me this is a picture of praise. The lion roars to intimidate but all we have to do is stand straight toward him and lift our hands and shout! This was Abraham praising God for Isacc before Isacc was even there. It's what we have to do when the devil roars in our face with a sickness. We begin to praise God for healing before healing is there because by His stripes we were healed. When the devil roars at our bank account, we begin to praise God that He is going to supply all our needs according to His riches and glory. When the devil roars to instill fear and anxiety, we praise God for the peace that passes all understanding. Remember he is 'like' a roaring lion but the real lion is on the inside of us: the Lion of Judah!

> *Immediately Jesus made His disciples get into the boat and go before Him to the other side, while He sent the multitudes*

away. And when He had sent the multitudes away, He went up on the mountain by Himself to pray. Now when evening came, He was alone there. But the boat was now in the middle of the sea, tossed by the waves, for the wind was contrary. Now in the fourth watch of the night Jesus went to them, walking on the sea. And when the disciples saw Him walking on the sea, they were troubled, saying, "It is a ghost!" And they cried out for fear. But immediately Jesus spoke to them, saying, "Be of good cheer! It is I; do not be afraid." And Peter answered Him and said, "Lord, if it is You, command me to come to You on the water." So He said, "Come." And when Peter had come down out of the boat, he walked on the water to go to Jesus. But when he saw that the wind was boisterous, he was afraid; and beginning to sink he cried out, saying, "Lord, save me!" And immediately Jesus stretched out His hand and caught him, and said to him, "O you of little faith, why did you doubt?" And when they got into the boat, the wind ceased. Then those who were in the boat came and worshiped Him, saying, "Truly You are the Son of God." (Matthew 14:22-33 NKJV)

Peter's story is one of my favorite Bible stories because it shows us what a man just like us can do with a little faith and the Word of God. You see, walking on water is impossible (even though I know you tried it as a kid). You don't get very far. In this story, we see a man do something that is impossible and had never been done before.

The key thing to look at in this story is what Peter said to Jesus before he got out of the boat. He said, "Lord, if that's you, tell me to come." When Jesus said "Come," the impossible became possible instantly. The Word of God makes miracles happen.

Does God Still Heal Today?

We have all heard this story and heard the message, "keep your eyes on Jesus and you won't fall". But look at this, Peter got out of a boat in the middle of the storm and did something no one had ever done before. This wasn't calm water with Jesus close to the boat. This was a storm in the middle of the sea and Peter asked to walk to Jesus! When Peter begins to sink, Jesus grabs him but then says, "you of little faith." How could Jesus accuse him of little faith when he literally just stepped out on water in a storm? We know that the faith of a mustard seed can move mountains. A mustard seed is the smallest of seeds! How can He say, "little faith"?

Then Jesus clarifies by saying "why did you doubt?" Peter had the faith to get out of the boat but "little faith" is not talking about the size of faith, but the duration. His faith didn't last for very long. We have the faith to step forward for healing but does it last past the second row back to your seat? Our faith for a miracle is strong unless it doesn't happen immediately. We need to have faith in the Word of God! Peter wasn't walking on the water because we know that's impossible. Peter was walking on the Word of God when Jesus said come! When the Bible says something, we can stand on it no matter how long it takes to manifest!

So Jesus said to them, "Because of your unbelief; for assuredly, I say to you, if you have faith as a mustard seed, you will say to this mountain, 'Move from here to there,' and it will move; and nothing will be impossible for you." (Matthew 17:20 NKJV)

CHAPTER 7

How To Pray

And when you pray, you shall not be like the hypocrites. For they love to pray standing in the synagogues and on the corners of the streets, that they may be seen by men. Assuredly, I say to you, they have their reward. But you, when you pray, go into your room, and when you have shut your door, pray to your Father who is in the secret place; and your Father who sees in secret will reward you openly. And when you pray, do not use vain repetitions as the heathen do. For they think that they will be heard for their many words. "Therefore do not be like them. For your Father knows the things you have need of before you ask Him. In this manner, therefore, pray: Our Father in heaven, Hallowed be Your name. Your kingdom come. Your will be done On earth as it is in heaven. Give us this day our daily bread. And forgive us our debts, As we forgive our debtors. And do not lead us into temptation, But deliver us from the evil one. For Yours is the kingdom and the power and the glory forever. Amen. (Matthew 6:5-13 NKJV)

I've had many people ask how to pray. Can you pray wrong? The answer is, yes. But thankfully Jesus taught His disciples how to pray so we can avoid praying incorrectly. And yet, I've heard many people pray just like Jesus spoke against. They use the same words over and over, as fast as they can, saying a bunch of random things, or even just getting lost in a prayer. Prayer doesn't need to be hard.

Jesus said to start prayer off by saying "Our Father." Does this mean you need to say this at the opening of every prayer? No, instead it means to keep in mind that we are asking our Father and not a stranger. When we realize God is our Father, we can pray differently. I would like to think we can ask our earthly father for something and not be afraid. At least, that is the way it should be. But regardless, the fact remains, you can ask your heavenly Father for something and expect Him to do it for you.

Then Jesus uses the phrase, "Your kingdom come. Your will be done On earth as it is in heaven." When we pray, pray what His will is. Everything in the Word that He has promised us, we can boldly pray as His will! Everything that is in heaven, we can pray on earth.

We need to be careful though, there is power in our words because of the dominion that God gave. We often say strange things instead of listening to what we are actually saying. How many times do we hear a service open up and start by saying, "Holy Spirit come into this place?" He already said I will never leave you nor forsake you; so what are we really saying? We have already been given the Spirit without measure. So instead we should say, "thank you for being here with me." It is important we don't just say random words but what God says. We should stop trying to get what God has already freely given. How often do we sing songs referring to wanting more of God? What does without measure mean? We could say I want to be more aware of You. We sing songs that say come rest on us (Old Testament) when He is inside of us (New Testament). Even at a young age the world teaches us that "words can't hurt you" or that "it's just a word". So we have people running around saying things like "that's sick", meaning something is good. You also hear "that's bad", "that's ill" and much more that is just "slang". We've taken words with a bad meaning and say them for good things now. We need to watch what we are saying.

Now don't take this wrong. Praying to just talk to God is different from praying over someone that is sick. God loves to hear our voice and spend time with us so don't start thinking "I'm not going to pray because I might say something wrong." We can ask our Father about anything but when praying for something that was already paid for we don't need to beg God but instead thank Him. How many times did Jesus "ask" God to heal? You might say, "But He is God." He was also fully man and functioning on earth. Did the disciples beg God to heal or did they command healing?

Then Peter said, "Silver and gold I do not have, but what I do have I give you: In the name of Jesus Christ of Nazareth, rise up and walk." (Acts 3:6 NKJV)

Then He called His twelve disciples together and gave them power and authority over all demons, and to cure diseases. He sent them to preach the kingdom of God and to heal the sick. (Luke 9:1-2 NKJV)

So they departed and went through the towns, preaching the gospel and healing everywhere. (Luke 9:6 NKJV)

And as you go, preach, saying, 'The kingdom of heaven is at hand.' Heal the sick, cleanse the lepers, raise the dead, cast out demons. Freely you have received, freely give. (Matthew 10:7-8 NKJV)

Now, Lord, look on their threats, and grant to Your servants that with all boldness they may speak Your word, by stretching out Your hand to heal, and that signs and wonders may be done through the name of Your holy Servant Jesus. (Acts 4:29-30 NKJV)

And through the hands of the apostles many signs and wonders were done among the people. And they were all with one accord in Solomon's Porch. (Acts 5:12 NKJV)

so that they brought the sick out into the streets and laid them on beds and couches, that at least the shadow of Peter passing by might fall on some of them. Also a multitude gathered from the surrounding cities to Jerusalem, bringing sick people and those who were tormented by unclean spirits, and they were all healed. (Acts 5:15-16 NKJV)

The disciples never begged God to do what Jesus already paid for! The disciples were only obedient to what Jesus told them. Jesus died, rose again, empowered them, and then sent them out.

Remember Mark 16, the great commission? We were all sent! It wasn't just the 12 disciples but all who believed! The difference is that we want to be loved by the world when Jesus said you will be hated for my name's sake. Why? Because, we should look just like Him. Jesus said if they hated me they will also hate you.

We see the disciples unafraid to preach and command healing and thus they saw results. Today, we don't want anyone to think we are crazy. We don't want people to dislike us. We don't want to heal the sick because what if it doesn't work. Did God ask them to pray and if it was His will they would be healed? No! Jesus didn't say "ask me," He said, "heal the sick!" This goes against most people's beliefs, but remember it is not our power but Christ living in us. Peter was very clear whose power it was after he told a man to get up and walk. He said "what I do have." After people were excited about what Peter did he pointed them back to the real power to heal!

So when Peter saw it, he responded to the people: "Men of Israel, why do you marvel at this? Or why look so intently at us, as though by our own power or godliness we had made this man walk? The God of Abraham, Isaac, and Jacob, the God of our fathers, glorified His Servant Jesus, whom you delivered up and denied in the presence of Pilate, when he was determined to let Him go. But you denied the Holy One and the Just, and asked for a murderer to be granted to you, and killed the Prince of life, whom God raised from the dead, of which we are witnesses. And His name, through faith in His name, has made this man strong, whom you see and know. Yes, the faith which comes through Him has given him this perfect soundness in the presence of you all. (Acts 3:12-16 NKJV)

When you realize that the Lord put the Holy Spirit in you because God wanted to touch the world, it will change your life.

When you understand dominion, you can pray differently with a confidence that something is going to happen.

It is important for us to understand the need to watch what comes out of our mouth. We haven't seen the amount of miracles that we should because we are doing it the way we think we should instead of looking at how the Bible commanded us. Instead of us speaking to the mountain to be removed we are telling God about the mountain. Then we get frustrated because the mountain didn't move when Jesus clearly said SPEAK to the mountain and it will be removed! We can try our way all we want and get frustrated but until you do what the Bible says you won't get Bible results.

Death and life are in the power of the tongue, And those who love it will eat its fruit. (Proverbs 18:21 NKJV)

I tell you, on the day of judgment people will give account for every careless word they speak. (Matthew 12:36 ESV)

Whoso keepeth his mouth and his tongue keepeth his soul from troubles. (Proverbs 21:23 KJV)

For we all stumble in many ways. And if anyone does not stumble in what he says, he is a perfect man, able also to bridle his whole body. If we put bits into the mouths of horses so that they obey us, we guide their whole bodies as well. Look at the ships also: though they are so large and are driven by strong winds, they are guided by a very small rudder wherever the will of the pilot directs. So also the tongue is a small member, yet it boasts of great things. How great a forest is set ablaze by such a small fire! (James 3:2-5 ESV)

Let the redeemed of the Lord say so, Whom He has redeemed from the hand of the enemy. (Psalms 107:2 NKJV)

Therefore, holy brethren, partakers of the heavenly calling, consider the Apostle and High Priest of our confession, Christ Jesus. (Hebrews 3:1 NKJV)

Seeing then that we have a great High Priest who has passed through the heavens, Jesus the Son of God, let us hold fast our confession. (Hebrews 4:14 NKJV)

We see in scripture, that not only is there power in our words but that Jesus is our High Priest. In Hebrews, it says He is the High Priest of our confession. Our confession is what we say. Jesus is the high priest of what we say.

What is a high priest? The high priest was the mediator between God and the people. No one could even go into the Holy of Holies back then because of sin, so the priest had to sacrifice for each person. This is why Jesus is our high priest once and for all. When God looks at us, He doesn't see our sins but the mediator, Jesus. So, if Jesus is the mediator between God and man, and the mediator of our confessions, we need to watch what comes out of our mouth!

There is life and death in the power of the tongue and many people are sick because they confess it every day. How many times have we heard someone claim their sickness by saying "my headaches," or, "my cancer is back," or "my back always hurts." Hebrews 10:23 tells us to hold fast our confession. How do we expect to get rid of any sickness while claiming it as our own? This sounds very double minded.

This is why so many people get prayed for, healed, and then seem to "lose" it the next week. We get healing and then the devil tries to bring a little pain to cause fear or doubt and see if we will confess it. There are many things in God's Word that we need to stand on for healing such as "the prayer of faith will raise up the sick", "lay hands on the sick and they will recover", and so much more. When sickness tries to come back, we need to remind ourselves we were healed in Jesus' name. We are no longer the sick trying to get healed but the healed resisting sickness.

And I will give you the keys of the kingdom of heaven, and whatever you bind on earth will be bound in heaven, and whatever you loose on earth will be loosed in heaven. (Matthew 16:19 NKJV)

Assuredly, I say to you, whatever you bind on earth will be bound in heaven, and whatever you loose on earth will be loosed in heaven. (Matthew 18:18 NKJV)

Jesus said that He gave us the keys to heaven and now it is up to us to bind on earth and also to loose. When was the last time we bound anything on earth or loosed anything? Why? It's in scripture? We would rather ask Him to do what He told us to do. When was the last time we spoke to a mountain to be removed? When was the last time we told a headache to leave in Jesus name?

People wonder why healing doesn't happen more often but I watch people and wonder why it happens as much as it does with the way people try and receive it. We need to be a generation that believes the Word and puts it into practice. We are still wondering if it's God's will to be healed and thinking He is the healer but maybe not today. Then when we finally get through all of that, we beg Him to do what He commanded us to do. We cannot go against the Word and expect to receive what's in it.

Think about this: someone finally gets a breakthrough and realizes it is God's will for healing because He already paid for healing. Then they go to pray and say stuff like, "God I know it's your will, I thank you for healing, I thank you that by your stripes I was healed in Jesus name." Although you might think this is a great prayer because you said a lot of scripture, said great things that are true about God, not one time did you speak to the mountain.

Again, we need to look at how Jesus and the disciples got results. You need to speak to cancer, speak to pain, speak to your mountains, and command them to leave in Jesus name. When Jesus said ask anything in my name and it will be done for you, He also said until now you have asked nothing in my name. Asking in His name isn't just saying "in the name of Jesus," it is understanding that asking in His name is the authority God gave us. Jesus is saying until now you've asked nothing in my name because the Holy Spirit wasn't living on the inside yet. With the Holy Spirit on the inside, the Word, and us believing it, we will get horsepower.

And war broke out in heaven: Michael and his angels fought with the dragon; and the dragon and his angels fought, but they did not prevail, nor was a place found for them in heaven any longer. So the great dragon was cast out, that serpent of old, called the Devil and Satan, who deceives the whole world; he was cast to the earth, and his angels were cast out with him. Then I heard a loud voice saying in heaven, "Now salvation, and strength, and the kingdom of our God, and the power of His Christ have come, for the accuser of our brethren, who accused them before our God day and night, has been cast down. And they overcame him by the blood of the Lamb and by the word of their testimony, and they did not love their lives to the death. Therefore rejoice, O heavens, and you who dwell in them! Woe to the inhabitants of the earth and the sea! For the devil has come down to you, having great wrath, because he knows that he has a short time."
(Revelation 12:7-12 NKJV)

Revelation 12 paints the picture of Satan being thrown out of heaven. As it goes on it actually talks about you and me winning. John saw you and me winning against the devil. He said they overcame him by the blood of the lamb and the word of their testimony! The blood of the lamb is what Jesus did and the word of their testimony is what we say. There is power in what you believe and what comes out of your mouth! Do not claim sickness when trying to be healed. Do not speak death when praying. Speak the Word and what God said and believe it.

CHAPTER 8

Does the Bible Have Stories Against Healing?

We've looked at many scriptures on healings, ways to be healed, and whether it is God's will for healing. But if we want to be absolutely accurate, we must be thorough and look at all scripture. Are there scriptures or stories in the Bible that indicate healing may sometimes not be God's will?

In order to answer this, first we will need to look at what we talked about in the beginning; rightly dividing truth. When you read scripture, make note of what covenant that passage was under; the Old Covenant or New Covenant.

Remember, if it is a passage from prior to Jesus dying and rising again, then it was under the Old Covenant. The Old Covenant was not just what was in the Old Testament but anything before Jesus rose from the dead. So, that means even the four gospels are 99% under the Old Covenant.

Second, look at who wrote the passage of scripture, what was said, and was it for us. The Bible is the Word of God but that does not mean that everything in there is directly for us to use as a literal example to live by. Some of the things are a record of history from which we can learn. You see accounts of the Israelites mistreating people which is obviously not an example of God's will for His people. In fact, the Hebrew people were rebuked on many occasions for doing things the Lord had instructed them not to.

Also, you see stories like Job's, where his wife tells Job he sinned and that he should curse God and die. This is very clearly not something we should do but it is recorded for us to learn from. Even the disciples, who were men of God, messed up many times and it's recorded for our benefit but not as an example of how to live, but rather an example of how to avoid making the same mistakes.

Understanding Job

Job is a perfect example of a story that is often used to say that God doesn't heal everyone. I've even heard people say that they are going through a "Job trial." Just because Job went through a trial does not mean God has created a "Job trial" for all of us to go through. If we want to learn the wisdom God has for us from the book of Job, we need to understand its context in relation to the rest of the Bible, who the author is, and who else is speaking throughout the book.

So, let's take a deeper look at some of this information. The story of Job is recorded by Elihu. We know that all scripture is inspired by God so regardless of who wrote the book, we can take what they wrote as inspired by God. Also, when God speaks, you can always apply it to your life!

Now consider this, Job (who is not the author) and His friends (who are also not the authors) are speaking for 29 out of 42 chapters of Job. These chapters are simply their recorded conversations, not necessarily the inspired Word of God. How do we know this? Because even though all scripture is inspired by God, they were not the author of the book but simply a part of the story being told. Not everyone who speaks in the Bible was speaking the inspired words of God. Think about characters like Pharaoh, Goliath, and even Satan is quoted in the Bible.

This is why it is important to note who the author (the inspired one) was. Thirteen chapters of the book are either God or the author (Elihu) speaking to help us understand the significance. Chapters 1-2 is narrative and sets the stage for where the story is taking place and who is important to the story. Chapters 3-31 are Job's friends giving him advice and telling him all this was because of sin in his life. Chapters 32-37 is where Elihu steps in and rebukes them all for what they are saying. Then, in Chapters 38-42 God speaks up, rebuking all of them for their ignorance.

Job is the one who said, "The Lord gave, and the Lord has taken away," yet we have turned this into a doctrine! The inspired word of God says that the gifts and the callings of God are irrevocable (Romans 11:29). This clearly shows us that He does not take away what He has given us. We even sing songs based on what Job said and forget that in Job 38 God rebuked Job and told him that Job doesn't even know what he is saying.

Then the LORD answered Job out of the whirlwind, and said: "Who is this who darkens counsel By words without knowledge? (Job 38:1,2 NKJV)

In Chapter 40:3-5, Job admits he was wrong:

"Shall the one who contends with the Almighty correct Him? He who rebukes God, let him answer it." Then Job answered the LORD and said: "Behold, I am vile; What shall I answer You? I lay my hand over my mouth. Once I have spoken, but I will not answer; Yes, twice, but I will proceed no further." (Job 40:2-5 NKJV)

And in Chapter 42, Job admits he didn't know:

You asked, 'Who is this who hides counsel without knowledge?' Therefore I have uttered what I did not understand, Things too wonderful for me, which I did not know. Listen, please, and let me speak; You said, 'I will question you, and you shall answer Me.' "I have heard of You by the hearing of the ear, But now my eye sees You. Therefore I abhor myself, And repent in dust and ashes." (Job 42:3-6 NKJV)

We also see in Chapter 42 that God tells Job's friends that what they said about Him to Job was completely wrong.

And so it was, after the LORD had spoken these words to Job, that the LORD said to Eliphaz the Temanite, "My wrath is aroused against you and your two friends, for you have not spoken of Me what is right, as My servant Job has. Now therefore, take for yourselves seven bulls and seven rams, go to My servant Job, and offer up for yourselves a burnt offering; and My servant Job shall pray for you. For I will accept him, lest I deal with you according to your folly; because you have not spoken of Me what is right, as

My servant Job has." So Eliphaz the Temanite and Bildad the Shuhite and Zophar the Naamathite went and did as the LORD commanded them; for the LORD had accepted Job. And the LORD restored Job's losses when he prayed for his friends. Indeed the LORD gave Job twice as much as he had before. (Job 42:7-10 NKJV)

The story of Job has been taught incorrectly so much that we get confused in church. The first thing that needs to be clear is this: God did not bring calamity on Job. The very first chapter in Job says that he was blessed among everyone at the time. He had God's favor all over him. But, Chapter 1:6-12 is where people get the teaching that God brought all the destruction on Job.

Now, there was a day when the sons of God came to present themselves before the LORD, and Satan came also among them. And the LORD said unto Satan, Whence comest thou? Then Satan answered the LORD, and said, From going to and fro in the earth, and from walking up and down in it. And the LORD said unto Satan, "Hast thou considered my servant Job, that there is none like him in the earth, a perfect and an upright man, one that feareth God, and escheweth evil?" Then Satan answered the LORD, and said, "Doth Job fear God for nought? Hast not thou made an hedge about him, and about his house, and about all that he hath on every side? thou hast blessed the work of his hands, and his substance is increased in the land. But put forth thine hand now, and touch all that he hath, and he will curse thee to thy face." And the LORD said unto Satan, "Behold, all that he hath is in thy power; only upon himself put not forth thine hand. So Satan went forth from the presence of the LORD." (Job 1:6-12 KJV)

There are a few things to look at in this passage. First, when the sons of God (angels) came to present themselves to God, Satan was there with them. Remember I mentioned before how Satan was kicked out of heaven, but now he was back there with the angels. God says, "Where have you been?" Then Satan says he was wandering on the earth. That kind of sounds like the devil walking about like a roaring lion seeking whom he may devour, doesn't it?

Then God says, "have you considered my servant Job?" This may seem like God is asking Satan to take a look at Job but this is a misunderstanding because of translation. A more literal translation of this scripture would be, "why are your eyes on my servant Job?" This changes the story quite a bit and is a more accurate interpretation from the Hebrew. God had noticed that Satan was already checking out Job because he was blessed by God more than everyone else.

Then, we think that God said, "okay, go test him to see what happens." That isn't what God said at all. He told Satan, "All that he has is in your hands." Why would God say that? Because of sin, Satan had our dominion and Jesus hadn't died yet. God was not giving permission to "go after Job" but rather He was stating the fact that "what Job had was already in his hands". But then God says not to take Job's life. All of this to say, things are lost in translation sometimes and it's good to study further. (*Andrew Wommack has a very detailed teaching on Job as well*)

And there was a day when his sons and his daughters were eating and drinking wine in their eldest brother's house: and there came a messenger unto Job, and said, The oxen were plowing, and the asses feeding beside them: and the Sabeans fell upon them, and took them away; yea, they have slain the servants with the edge of the sword; and I only am escaped alone to tell thee. While he was yet speaking, there came also another, and said, The fire of God is fallen from heaven, and hath burned up the sheep, and the servants, and consumed them; and I only am escaped alone to tell thee. While he was yet speaking, there came also another, and said, The Chaldeans made out three bands, and fell upon the camels, and have carried them away, yea, and slain the servants with the edge of the sword; and I only am escaped alone to tell thee. While he was yet speaking, there came also another, and said, Thy sons and thy daughters were eating and drinking wine in their eldest brother's house: and, behold, there came a great wind from the wilderness, and smote the four corners of the house, and it fell upon the young men, and they are dead; and I only am escaped alone to tell thee. Then Job arose, and rent his mantle, and shaved his head, and fell down upon the ground, and worshiped, and said, Naked came I out of my mother's womb, and naked shall I return thither: the LORD gave, and the LORD hath taken away; blessed be the name of the LORD. In all this Job sinned not, nor charged God foolishly. (Job 1:13-22 KJV)

Remember when we talked about how both faith and fear can create? The book of Job is a perfect example of this. In Job 1:13-22, it says that Job was afraid for his children and would often offer sacrifices for them in case they had sinned. Let me tell you, if Job was in fear that his kids might be sinning every night, they were probably sinning every night!

Also, remember that Jesus hadn't died yet so Job's kids were not under grace. Then Job says, "the thing which I greatly feared is come upon me..." God did not bring any of this on Job. When you break down scripture, it becomes clear that it was sin, fear, and the devil targeting Job because of God's favor on him that brought destruction into his life.

Also remember, after Job went through all this and still did not sin, God blessed him with double and Job lived another 140 years. Next time you think you are going through a "Job trial," get out of fear, remember who you are in Christ, and that you have the blood of Jesus covering you now! If you really are going through a "Job trial," you should praise God that there is going to be a double blessing on the other side of the trial. This does not mean God is the one who brings trials to you but that He will restore double if the devil is attacking you.

The devil attacked Job to completely destroy him and it did hurt Job but in the book of Luke, Satan tried to do the same thing again but it looked different.

And the Lord said, "Simon, Simon! Indeed, Satan has asked for you, that he may sift you as wheat. But I have prayed for you, that your faith should not fail; and when you have returned to Me, strengthen your brethren." (Luke 22:31,32 NKJV)

Simon had an intercessor but Job did not. Job is a story often used as an example for the doctrine that God brings sickness on us to teach us different things and keep us humble. This is not Biblical and is bad doctrine. God did not bring this on Job and doubly blessed him after his suffering. Sickness does not teach us; the Holy Spirit does. Sickness is of the devil who is here only to steal, kill, and destroy. Even in the Old Testament before Jesus, sickness was always part of the curse and never part of the blessing God wanted for His people. God never speaks of sickness in His word as something that is there to help us.

The Thorn in Paul's Flesh

Another example from scripture that people wrongly use to say, "God doesn't always heal" is Paul and his thorn-in-the-flesh. There are a few things we need to look at. What is a "thorn in the flesh?" Who was Paul? And what was God's answer?

And lest I should be exalted above measure by the abundance of the revelations, a thorn in the flesh was given to me, a messenger of Satan to buffet me, lest I be exalted above measure. Concerning this thing I pleaded with the Lord three times that it might depart from me. And He said to me, "My grace is sufficient for you, for My strength is made perfect in weakness." Therefore most gladly I will rather boast in my infirmities, that the power of Christ may rest upon me. Therefore I take pleasure in infirmities, in reproaches, in needs, in persecutions, in distresses, for Christ's sake. For when I am weak, then I am strong. (2 Corinthians 12:7-10 NKJV)

I have heard many preachers use this scripture to preach that you need to stay humble or God will take things from you. I have also heard that this was Paul asking for healing and God saying "no." Now, both of these interpretations contradict other scriptures and I don't believe the Bible contradicts itself, so there must be something else the Word is saying.

Second Corinthians 12:7 starts out by saying, "a thorn in the flesh was given to me" but then it goes on to say "a messenger of satan." So, on that alone, we can throw out that this was something that God gave to Paul. This was from Satan. God is never working WITH the devil for any reason. He will not bring you a messenger of Satan to teach you anything.

Satan is evil and we know that a messenger of Satan is obviously also evil. As a father, I would never bring evil to my kids to teach them a lesson. I wouldn't bring them drugs to teach them why drugs are bad. The same is true for our Heavenly Father. He is good and does not bring evil to us to teach us. Thus clearly this was not from God in any way, shape, or form!

The passage also says that Paul had an "abundance of revelation." This means Satan sent this messenger because he was fighting the revelation that would eventually become the New Testament as we know it today. The devil was trying to stop the Word from going forth! This reason for Paul's thorn-in-the-flesh is much more consistent with the devil's character than it is with God's according to scripture. So, let's not blame God for the devil's attacks.

Now we need to know what a thorn-in-the-flesh is, generally speaking. Some people believe it was a sickness with which Paul was afflicted. They say things like, "Paul often traveled with Luke who was a doctor, so Paul was probably sick because of all the sick people he was around." This is a strange assumption to make and takes a lot of guessing.

Another key factor in understanding this passage is knowing who Paul was. When Paul argued in the temple, he said he was a Pharisee among Pharisees. A Pharisee was someone who would study and memorize scripture (or the Old Testament). This means Paul knew the Old Testament very well. So, let's look at the Old Testament to see what it calls a thorn-in-the-flesh.

But if you do not drive out the inhabitants of the land from before you, then it shall be that those whom you let remain shall be irritants in your eyes and <u>thorns in your sides,</u> and they shall harass you in the land where you dwell. (Numbers 33:55 NKJV)

Know for certain that the LORD your God will no longer drive out these nations from before you. But they shall be snares and traps to you, and <u>scourges on your sides and thorns in your eyes,</u> until you perish from this good land which the LORD your God has given you. (Joshua 23:13 NKJV)

Therefore I also said, 'I will not drive them out before you; but they shall be <u>thorns in your side,</u> and their gods shall be a snare to you.' " (Judges 2:3 NKJV)

Every time the Old Testament refers to this kind of "thorn" it's talking about persecution from those that hated God's people. The Israelites were constantly attacked and mistreated by surrounding countries because of God's favor. Is it possible that Paul was talking about persecution when he wrote about the thorn in his flesh? Could it be possible that Satan kept bringing persecution against Paul to stop his preaching and stop him from writing the Bible? This seems a lot more consistent with the other accounts that Paul wrote.

I say again, let no one think me a fool. If otherwise, at least receive me as a fool, that I also may boast a little. What I speak, I speak not according to the Lord, but as it were, foolishly, in this confidence of boasting. Seeing that many boast according to the flesh, I also will boast. For you put up with fools gladly, since you yourselves are wise! For you put up with it if one brings you into bondage, if one devours you, if one takes from you, if one exalts himself, if one strikes you on the face. To our shame I say that we were too weak for that! But in whatever anyone is bold—I speak foolishly—I am bold also. (2 Corinthians 11:16-21 NKJV)

Are they Hebrews? So am I. Are they Israelites? So am I. Are they the seed of Abraham? So am I. Are they ministers of Christ?—I speak as a fool—I am more: in labors more abundant, in stripes above measure, in prisons more frequently, in deaths often. From the Jews five times I received forty stripes minus one. Three times I was beaten with rods; once I was stoned; three times I was shipwrecked; a night and a day I have been in the deep; in journeys often, in perils of waters, in perils of robbers, in perils of my own countrymen, in perils of the Gentiles, in perils in the city, in perils in the wilderness, in perils in the sea, in perils among false brethren; in weariness and toil, in sleeplessness often, in hunger and thirst, in fastings often, in cold and nakedness— besides the other things, what comes upon me daily: my deep concern for all the churches. Who is weak, and I am not weak? Who is made to stumble, and I do not burn with indignation? If I must boast, I will boast in the things which concern my infirmity. The God and Father of our Lord Jesus Christ, who is blessed forever, knows that I am not lying. In Damascus the governor, under Aretas the king, was guarding the city of the Damascenes with a garrison, desiring to arrest me; but I was let down in a basket through a window in the wall, and escaped from his hands. (2 Corinthians 11:22-33 NKJV)

Paul was persecuted for the message he was preaching wherever he went and it sounds like Paul was very bold about the persecutions he went through for preaching the gospel. In every other aspect of his life, Paul displayed humility. But it seems like this was the one thing he was "proud" of. This makes so much more sense then God trying to use any sickness to keep him humble!

So, finally take note of the fact that Paul prayed three times for this to be taken away from him. Why would God not take it away? There is only one thing we are not redeemed from by the cross and that is persecution.

Remember the word that I said to you, 'A servant is not greater than his master.' If they persecuted Me, they will also

persecute you. If they kept My word, they will keep yours
also. (John 15:20 NKJV)

Do not marvel, my brethren, if the world hates you.
(1 John 3:13 NKJV)

If the world hates you, you know that it hated Me before
it hated you. If you were of the world, the world would love its
own. Yet because you are not of the world, but I chose you out of
the world, therefore the world hates you. Remember the word that
I said to you, 'A servant is not greater than his master.' If they
persecuted Me, they will also persecute you. If they kept My word,
they will keep yours also. But all these things they will do to you
for My name's sake, because they do not know Him who sent Me.
If I had not come and spoken to them, they would have no sin, but
now they have no excuse for their sin. He who hates Me hates My
Father also. If I had not done among them the works which no one
else did, they would have no sin; but now they have seen and also
hated both Me and My Father. But this happened that the word
might be fulfilled which is written in their law, 'They hated Me
without a cause.' (John 15:18-25 NKJV)

These things I have spoken to you, that in Me you may
have peace. In the world you will have tribulation; but be of good
cheer, I have overcome the world. (John 16:33 NKJV)

So, these passages show us that not only are we not
promised to be delivered from persecution but we are guaranteed
that it will come! "In this world you will have trouble." This is

why bad things happen to good people. If you look like Jesus then you are going to be hated because they hated Him!

We should be acting like Jesus in the same way Paul was acting like Jesus. Paul said, "follow me as I follow Christ." In other words, "I look like Jesus and so should you." This is why Paul had a thorn in his flesh! He looked like Jesus. The thorn-in-his-flesh didn't mean he couldn't get healed; it meant that people hated him because of the gospel.

So, go back to 2 Corinthians 12 and let's address one more misconception about this passage. When Paul prayed and asked God to take away the thorn three times, God's reply was not a "no!" God said, "my Grace is sufficient for you!" His Grace is all we need. Grace is everything that Jesus paid for on the cross. Grace is that Shalom we talked about. Grace is Jesus. That is all you need in order to make it through the persecution that will come against you because of the gospel.

God didn't say "no," He said "yes" and gave Paul the answer. Grace is all that is needed to get through the troubles of life. How do we access this grace? By faith! Grace without faith doesn't work and neither does faith without grace. You can only have faith for what was already provided by grace. You can "believe" in whatever you want but results will only happen when it's belief in what Jesus has promised. If you are "believing" you will win the lottery, you might be disappointed. If you have faith in people, they will let you down. But you can have faith in God's grace, Shalom, Jesus, and everything that was paid for on the cross. It will never let you down. If it's in the Word you can have faith in it and you will not be disappointed.

On the other side though, grace is there even without faith. But although it is paid for and a done deal, you will never access it without faith. The Word is clear that grace operates through faith. If it was not through faith then anyone and everyone could go to heaven. The Word says you have to believe in your heart and confess with your mouth then you will be saved. It's not just, "Jesus paid for it and so everyone gets it no matter what." If you want to receive anything that is included in grace, you can only do it by faith.

We also know that faith comes by hearing, and hearing by the Word of God, so we can renew our mind to have more faith for any part of grace. Some people have the faith for salvation but not for healing. Some people have faith for healing but not blessing. Every part of grace can be accessed through faith.

When Paul asked to be released from this thorn in the flesh, God told him that grace was all he needed and it was enough to get him through. Paul goes on to explain even more by saying, *"Therefore most gladly I will rather boast in my infirmities, that the power of Christ may rest upon me. Therefore I take pleasure in infirmities, in reproaches, in needs, in persecutions, in distresses, for Christ's sake. For when I am weak, then I am strong."* When you are weak He is strong which means, when you can't, He can. His grace is sufficient to get you through. This was not Paul sick, trying to be healed, and God saying "no." This was Paul under attack from Satan because of the Gospel and God saying "yes, I am here for you and already paid for it!"

CHAPTER 9

Are You Going to Fight or Cooperate with the Devil?

This chapter may be hard for some because it shines a light on the problem and shows us our responsibility. We went through Hosea 4:6 early, which says, *"My people are destroyed for lack of knowledge. Because you have rejected knowledge, I also will reject you from being priest for Me; Because you have forgotten the law of your God, I also will forget your children."* People are dying everyday because of what they don't understand. If we don't spend time in the Word, how can the Word change our situation? Faith comes by hearing the Word of God but if we don't even know what the word says we cannot have faith in it. And so we are destroyed.

Not only do we not study the Word but we pay lots of money to be distracted by things outside of it. How much time do we spend on our phone, watching tv, listening to music, or whatever else you enjoy? These things are not all bad but most of the time they contain a message that is opposite of scripture and reflects the world. Every time you turn on the TV, it's talking about a new virus coming, flu season, wars, a natural disaster, and so on. It's hard to stay in faith when constantly feeding fear. Whatever we feed grows and we pay money for entertainment to feed us fear. I am not saying to pretend that what is happening in the world doesn't exist but I would rather know what the Word says over what the world says.

For we do not wrestle against flesh and blood, but against principalities, against powers, against the rulers of the darkness of this age, against spiritual hosts of wickedness in the heavenly places. (Ephesians 6:12 NKJV)

Did you ever notice that many of the healing miracles that Jesus did he didn't command healing but instead cast out a demon and then the individual was healed? Does this mean every time we are sick, we have a demon? Obviously not, but we cannot overlook the scriptures and how Jesus healed sometimes. We need to be filled with the Spirit so we know when to command healing or cast out a demon. In about half of the miracles Jesus did, He cast demons out and sickness went with them. If Jesus did miracles this way that often, we may want to pay attention to that.

There is also a debate in the church about whether you can be a Christian and have a demon tormenting you. I don't want to go down the road on whether you can be a Christian and possessed or just tormented. All I know is I've had to cast demons out of some good Christian people before. Anything like fear, sin, even what we put in front of our eyes, can open up doors we maybe didn't want opened. This is why it is so important to keep sin out of our life! Yes, Jesus paid for sin on the cross but we also need to realize that the devil still operates through sin. So if we live in sin (not just make a mistake), it opens the door to Satan.

This is why even just putting certain things in front of our eyes is dangerous. People that watch horror movies wonder why they live in fear. Those that give into addictions give control to the addiction and open a door for the enemy's destruction in so many different ways.

This chapter's title asks, "are you cooperating with the devil?" You could be cooperating without even realizing it. Remember, it's what we **don't** know that **will** get us killed. So, cooperating unknowingly is just as bad. When we open doors through sin, put ungodly things in front of us, or just live in fear, we are cooperating with the devil.

When we cooperate with the devil, we are believing a lie! Consider Adam and Eve. They didn't just come up with the idea to eat the forbidden fruit out of nowhere. They first decided to listen to a lie, then it led to sin. This world teaches us "we're only human" when the truth for believers is that with the Holy Spirit we are so much more.

Believing we are only human is listening to a lie. We think, "Well, I'm getting older and my body just breaks down." That line of thinking is cooperating with a lie. The Bible says that Moses's eyes were not dim in his old age. This means he was still in good health all the way up until death.

Every day, we are taught about a new sickness to watch out for but the Bible says no plague will come near our house. Why don't we believe that? The devil loves to put pain and sickness on people, so because we feel the tremors of his attacks we begin to doubt the Word based on our experiences. When we listen to a lie, we unknowingly cooperate with the devil.

For most of us, there is at least one idea we believe that isn't in the Bible. Sin is an obvious example of our actions not lining up with what the Bible says but the Word also says anything not done in faith is sin. There are a lot of things that many believers have almost forgotten are sin. Envy is a huge one. When we are self-seeking or have envy in our life it can cause confusion and every evil thing.

For where envy and self-seeking exist, confusion and every evil thing are there. (James 3:16 NKJV)

En·vy, (noun)
a feeling of discontented or resentful longing aroused
by someone else's possessions, qualities, or luck.

Every evil thing is there. That is a sobering statement for the person who has envy in their life. These are the open doors I am talking about. Sometimes we are opening up doors that we don't even know. We don't think of envy as one of the major sins. Being discontent or resentful doesn't seem big, but the Bible is clear that every evil thing is there.

We think of stealing, murder, or adultery as being the horrid sins and they are, but all of those start with being discontent. Jesus is the only one that can satisfy what we are lacking on the inside. When we don't understand that, we look at others and compare ourselves, judge those around us, and are discontent. We then think we are discontent with others when we are really discontent with our relationship with the Lord. This is where sin begins. This is why Paul said to be content in all things. It didn't matter if he was shipwrecked, in prison, or being stoned, Paul was in the Spirit. We cannot be content if we do not have the Holy Spirit. So, to stay out of envy and self-seeking we need to stay in the Spirit!

But I rejoiced in the Lord greatly that now at last your care for me has flourished again; though you surely did care, but you lacked opportunity. Not that I speak in regard to need, for I have learned in whatever state I am, to be content: I know how to be abased, and I know how to abound. Everywhere and in all things I have learned both to be full and to be hungry, both to abound and to suffer need. I can do all things through Christ who strengthens me. (Philippians 4:10-13 NKJV)

Therefore submit to God. Resist the devil and he will flee from you. (James 4:7 NKJV)

You Must Resist

In James 4:7 the Word tells us to resist the devil and he will flee. Most people allow the devil to come in and then ask everyone else to pray that he leaves them alone instead of just resisting him in the first place. Many people want to mess with stuff they shouldn't then they want the blessings of God to flow. Remember, he walks around like a roaring lion seeking whom he may devour. We have more authority in our pinky than the devil has but most people want to play with sin and wonder why life isn't working the way it should. We need to resist temptation not mess with it. The devil and demons only have the authority we give to them.

When He had come to the other side, to the country of the Gergesenes, there met Him two demon-possessed men, coming out of the tombs, exceedingly fierce, so that no one could pass that way. And suddenly they cried out, saying, "What have we to do with You, Jesus, You Son of God? Have You come here to torment us before the time?" Now a good way off from them there was a herd of many swine feeding. So the demons begged Him, saying, "If You cast us out, permit us to go away into the herd of swine." And He said to them, "Go." So when they had come out, they went into the herd of swine. And suddenly the whole herd of swine ran violently down the steep place into the sea, and perished in the water. Then those who kept them fled; and they went away into the city and told everything, including what had happened to the demon-possessed men. And behold, the whole city came out to meet Jesus. And when they saw Him, they begged Him to depart from their region.
Matthew 8:28-34 NKJV

The demons didn't even have authority to go into the pigs! They needed Jesus' permission. Demons do not have a foothold on you (if you are a Christian) without an open door. If you are not a Christian, without the blood of Jesus, then that is different. With the blood of Jesus in our life we must give control in order for demons to have a place.

Remember, that demons want to take control and overpower us but the Holy Spirit wants to empower us. When we give demons control through open doors, sickness can come on our body. This is not the case every time someone is sick; remember we need the Holy Spirit to discern. When people want to move in a spiritual gift like healing, tongues, prophecy or any of the gifts of the Spirit they want the Holy Spirit to take control of their body. The Holy Spirit will not make your mouth move and you start praying in the spirit or take control of your body so you go and pray with someone for healing. The Holy Spirit will empower you and lead you. All of the gifts work with obedience and faith! Again demons want to over power you and the Holy Spirit will empower you!

But consider this; in Deuteronomy 28, sickness was part of the curse and not part of the blessing. Today, with the blood of Jesus, we have been redeemed from the curse but that doesn't mean the curse isn't still there if we want to accept it. The Devil would love nothing more than to keep us under the law and the curse. When he offers sickness, don't take it. We have free will and we need to choose the things of God.

I call heaven and earth as witnesses today against you, that I have set before you life and death, blessing and cursing; therefore choose life, that both you and your descendants may live; (Deuteronomy 30:19 NKJV)

We have free will and God says here are the choices: life and death. Then He makes it easy and gives us the answer. He says, "choose life." We live in a world that the devil is running but through the blood of Jesus we can take back that authority.

We are called to fight and take back what the enemy stole. We should not just let him put whatever he wants on us. We have the blood of Jesus. To fight back and not cooperate with the devil, is to not believe his lies but only what the Word says. We are to be like Jesus in this world.

Love has been perfected among us in this: that we may have boldness in the day of judgment; because as He is, so are we in this world. (1 John 4:17 NKJV)

I am the true vine, and My Father is the vinedresser. Every branch in Me that does not bear fruit He takes away; and every branch that bears fruit He prunes, that it may bear more fruit. You are already clean because of the word which I have spoken to you. Abide in Me, and I in you. As the branch cannot bear fruit of itself, unless it abides in the vine, neither can you, unless you abide in Me. I am the vine, you are the branches. He who abides in Me, and I in him, bears much fruit; for without Me you can do nothing. If anyone does not abide in Me, he is cast out as a branch and is withered; and they gather them and throw them into the fire, and they are burned. If you abide in Me, and My words abide in you, you will ask what you desire, and it shall be done for you. By this My Father is glorified, that you bear much fruit; so you will be My disciples. (John 15:1-8 NKJV)

The only way to fight back is by realizing you are like Jesus. Remember, without Jesus we are nothing, but thank God we are not without Him. John 15 uses the analogy of a vine and branches. Remember, that Jesus is our high priest, the mediator between God and man. This is why He is the vine. God is the source of everything so He would be the root. We, as Christians, are called the branches. The vine connects the root to the branches. Every good thing from the root flows to the branches through the vine. Without the root, the branches would die. Without the vine, the branches would die. But look at where the fruit grows.

We are the branches but we bear the fruit of God in our lives. The sweet fruit of the spirit should be coming through us. This happens only if we abide in Him like John 15 says. It even says that God is glorified through us bearing much fruit! All the fruit in our life shouldn't be to glorify ourselves but Him! Every good thing in our life should point to Jesus!

We need to stop cooperating with the devil (even unknowingly) and start realizing we are one with Christ. And the way to do this is by studying intently the perfect law, His word. All things that the Father has, Jesus has and the Holy Spirit takes what is Jesus' and declares it to us! So, we have the fruit! There are gifts of the Spirit and there are fruits of the Spirit. The fruit of the Spirit is what the Holy Spirit wants to do in you. The gifts of the Spirit is what the Holy Spirit wants to do through you! He wants to use us!

However, when He, the Spirit of truth, has come, He will guide you into all truth; for He will not speak on His own authority, but whatever He hears He will speak; and He will tell you things to come. He will glorify Me, for He will take of what is Mine and declare it to you. All things that the Father has are Mine. Therefore I said that He will take of Mine and declare it to you. (John 16:13-15 NKJV)

Final Thoughts

There is so much we can learn about healing as we continue to grow. We must never assume we know all there is to know about God's kingdom system in any capacity. He is God and He will always be above and beyond what we can think but the Holy Spirit will continue to teach us "all things." We have to continue going to scripture for better understanding and I hope this book has helped with that some. I pray that you have received new revelation or revival of dormant faith by reading this.

We need people free and Jesus paid a high price for us to be free! We need to take advantage of everything that was paid for on the cross, find all the promises in scripture, and put our faith in them. The main point of this book is not only to teach healing but also to stir up your faith in the Word!

Faith is the way to access whatever you need but we live in a generation that neglects spending time with God. We cannot build faith without spending time studying His word that tells how to build it. The Bible has the answers to life and victory so it would make sense for everyone to spend time digging into it. Yet many people turn to self-help books instead when they can have the Helper (Holy Spirit) on the inside. So many people struggle with depression and anxiety when they can have the peace that passes all understanding. People struggle with finances when God said He would provide for all our needs, not just according to our needs, but according to His riches in glory! People struggle with sickness without realizing that by His stripes we were (that is past tense) healed.

Grace and peace be multiplied to you in the knowledge of God and of Jesus our Lord, as His divine power has given to us all things that pertain to life and godliness, through the knowledge of Him who called us by glory and virtue, by which have been given to us exceedingly great and precious promises, that through these you may be partakers of the divine nature, having escaped the corruption that is in the world through lust. (2 Peter 1:2-4 NKJV)

Now to Him who is able to do exceedingly abundantly above all that we ask or think, according to the power that works in us. (Ephesians 3:20 NKJV)

We know that God is the only one that is able to do exceedingly abundantly above all we can ask or think; but it says according to the power that works in **us**! Most Christians don't believe that. They think it is all up to God and that He will just do whatever He wants to do. But no, we have a part to play!

Does God still heal today? Yes, but maybe not the way most people think. We are after-the-cross New Covenant believers. So we should not be begging God to do something He already did but rather receiving our miracle that He already paid for through faith!

We need to believe what the Word says and receive what Jesus did the way He commanded us to receive it. We realize we wrestle not against flesh and blood but against the devil who is looking to steal, kill, and destroy. We realize that greater is He that is in us than he that is in the world. We recognize that God sent Jesus as a man because He gave dominion to man. We know that through what Jesus did on the cross we are now qualified to receive the free gift of the Holy Spirit which gives us power to trample the works of the enemy.

We realize that God wanted the Holy Spirit in us not just to make us emotional but so He could touch the world through us as His hands and feet. Jesus not only gave us the Holy Spirit but commanded us to go out into all the world. We use our words and authority like Jesus did to speak to the mountain so the mountain will be moved. We do not need to tell God about the mountain but rather believe Him when He told **us** to speak to the mountain.

We realize that God told us whatever we bind is bound and whatever we lose is losed.
We believe that with the Holy Spirit living in us we have the same power that raised Christ from the dead on the inside of us.
We believe Matthew 10:1 when Jesus called the disciples to Him and gave them power over every unclean spirit and over every kind of sickness and over every kind of disease.

We know that it is not only God's will for healing but that Jesus already paid for it and He went about healing them all! Healing isn't just something He does, it's who He is! He is the same yesterday, today, and forever. He is Jehovah Rapha the God that heals!

VERSES FOR HEALING

"Heal me, O Lord, and I will be healed; save me and I will be saved, for you are the one I praise." ~ Jeremiah 17:14

"Is anyone among you sick? Let them call the elders of the church to pray over them and anoint them with oil in the name of the Lord. And the prayer offered in faith will make the sick person well; the Lord will raise them up. If they have sinned, they will be forgiven." ~ James 5:14-15

"He said, "If you listen carefully to the LORD your God and do what is right in his eyes, if you pay attention to his commands and keep all his decrees, I will not bring on you any of the diseases I brought on the Egyptians, for I am the LORD, who heals you." ~ Exodus 15:26

"Worship the LORD your God, and his blessing will be on your food and water. I will take away sickness from among you..." ~ Exodus 23:25

"So do not fear, for I am with you; do not be dismayed, for I am your God. I will strengthen you and

help you; I will uphold you with my righteous right hand." ~ Isaiah 41:10

"Surely he took up our pain and bore our suffering, yet we considered him punished by God, stricken by him, and afflicted. But he was pierced for our transgressions, he was crushed for our iniquities; the punishment that brought us peace was on him, and by his wounds we are healed." ~ Isaiah 53:4-5

"But I will restore you to health and heal your wounds,' declares the LORD" ~ Jeremiah 30:17

"See now that I myself am he! There is no god besides me. I put to death and I bring to life, I have wounded and I will heal, and no one can deliver out of my hand." ~ Deuteronomy 32:39

"You restored me to health and let me live. Surely it was for my benefit that I suffered such anguish. In your love you kept me from the pit of destruction; you have put all my sins behind your back." ~ Isaiah 38:16-17

"I have seen their ways, but I will heal them; I will guide them and restore comfort to Israel's mourners, creating praise on their lips. Peace, peace, to those far and near," says the LORD. "And I will heal them." ~ Isaiah 57:18-19

"Nevertheless, I will bring health and healing to it; I will heal my people and will let them enjoy abundant peace and security." ~ Jeremiah 33:6

"Dear friend, I pray that you may enjoy good health and that all may go well with you, even as your soul is getting along well." ~ 3 John 1:2

"And my God will meet all your needs according to the riches of his glory in Christ Jesus." ~ Philippians 4:19

"He will wipe every tear from their eyes. There will be no more death' or mourning or crying or pain, for the old order of things has passed away." ~ Revelations 21:4

REFERENCES

Lindsey, Peter (May 13, 2021). *The Complexity of Lion Roars.* https://lionrecoveryfund.org/the-complexity-of-lion-roars/

Unknown (Last Updated: December 21, 2022). *How to Survive a Lion Attack.* https://www.wikihow.com/Survive-a-Lion-Attack

Qamar M. F., Raza I (2012). *Scientific evidences that pig meat (pork) is prohibited for human health.* Scientific Papers. Series D. Animal Science, Vol. LV, ISSN-L 2285-5750, 281-286. https://animalsciencejournal.usamv.ro/index.php/scientific-papers/131-a56#spucontentCitation56

Made in the USA
Columbia, SC
26 November 2024

47094727R00087